Equality of Opportunity for Sexual and Gender Minorities 2024

A reproducibility package is available for this
book in the Reproducible Research Repository at
https://reproducibility.worldbank.org/index.php/catalog/182.

Equality of Opportunity for Sexual and Gender Minorities 2024

WORLD BANK GROUP

Contents

Contents

Contents

Appendixes

Boxes

Figures

Contents

Maps

Tables

Contents

Foreword

The World Bank is committed to supporting countries in efforts to advance inclusion that benefits all, including sexual and gender minorities. In recent years, many countries have made advances in this area through the adoption of laws and policies that promote inclusion and protect against discrimination based on sexual orientation, gender identity and expression, and sex characteristics (SOGIESC). Around the globe, however, sexual and gender minorities continue to face daunting challenges to inclusion, and these challenges are grounded in stigma, discrimination, and—too often—violence.

Within this context, *Equality of Opportunity for Sexual and Gender Minorities 2024* (EQOSOGI) aims to contribute to the evidence base for SOGIESC inclusion. All too often, a lack of SOGIESC-specific quantitative and qualitative data hinders efforts at policy and program reform to address the exclusion of sexual and gender minorities. This report helps to overcome that data gap through an extensive analysis of the legal status of sexual and gender minorities in 64 countries that vary in geography, income levels, and degrees of commitment to inclusion.

This report—a significant expansion on the first EQOSOGI report that assessed 16 countries—explores areas such as education, employment, and access to services, with the aim of informing legislative reform and supporting research that leads to positive development outcomes. The findings underscore the importance of inclusive policies and laws for a country's economic development, highlight the correlation between SOGIESC inclusion and economic growth, and provide insights into the legal frameworks that govern the lived experience of sexual and gender minorities. The report acknowledges that, despite progress, no country has fully achieved equality under the law for sexual and gender minorities. But the report also shines a light on good practices among the sample countries, which we do with the intent of advancing to the broader goal of inclusive and sustainable economic development.

This report is an example of the work under way at the World Bank to develop expertise and generate analysis to deepen the understanding of the challenges to equality of opportunity that sexual and gender minorities encounter. It will inform our support to borrowing countries in their efforts to address discrimination through design and implementation of World Bank–financed projects. Our hope is that other stakeholders and actors will benefit from this report as well.

Foreword

By providing sexual and gender minorities with enabling legal and policy environments, countries can strengthen social cohesion and build more resilient and sustainable communities. Ultimately, inclusion and ensuring equality of opportunity for sexual and gender minorities is a development strategy that benefits everyone.

Juergen Voegele
Vice President, Sustainable Development
The World Bank

Acknowledgments

Data collection and analysis for the *Equality of Opportunity for Sexual and Gender Minorities 2024* report were conducted by a World Bank Group team led jointly by Clifton Cortez (Sexual Orientation and Gender Identity Global Advisor) and Julia Constanze Braunmiller (Senior Private Sector Development Specialist, Development Economics).

Samreen Shahbaz assisted in coordination of the project and supervised the legal data collection and analysis. Paola Ballon led and supervised the economic analysis. Other members of the core research team were Omar Alburqueque Chavez, Lucia Arnal Rodriguez, Jessica Chilin Hernandez, Christian de la Medina Soto, Gudrun Jevne, Hicham Kantar, Sontia Sophie Nkenkeu Keck, and Stephen Winkler. The team was assisted by Elizabeth Acul, John (Ioannis) Arzinos, Ben Bakalovic, Aieshwarya Davis, Alessandro Di Rosa, Karolina Ordon, and Razilya Shakirova.

The team is grateful for valuable comments from colleagues, both within and outside the World Bank Group, who supported the initiative and provided invaluable technical assistance on the connection between equality legislation and economic development. The study was peer-reviewed by Isis Gaddis (Senior Economist, SSAS1), Hillary C. Johnson (Economist, EAPCE), Remi D. Moncel (Senior Counsel, LEGEN), Valeria Perotti (Manager, DECBE), Yana van der Meulen Rodgers (Professor and Faculty Director, Rutgers School of Management and Labor Relations), and Kees Waaldijk (Professor of Comparative Sexual Orientation Law, Leiden University).

The report was edited by Sabra Ledent and Honora Mara. Jihane El Khoury Roederer was the principal graphic designer. The team also thanks Stephen Pazdan and Jewel McFadden for managing the publication process with the World Bank's publishing program. The *Equality of Opportunity for Sexual and Gender Minorities 2024* communication and outreach strategy is led by a team composed of Carl Hanlon, Laura Ivers, and Edy Semaan as well as World Bank Group External and Corporate Relations colleagues at headquarters and around the world.

The team also thanks the World Bank Country Management Units for their valuable contributions and reviews of the countries covered in the report. The initiative is also supported by a collaboration with the Asian Development Bank, which conducted data collection and analysis in 17 countries in Asia (Central, East, South, and Southeast).

This initiative benefited greatly from consultation with and advice from the staff at the International Lesbian, Gay, Bisexual, Trans, and Intersex Association (ILGA World); ILGA-Europe; the Franklin & Marshall Global Barometers; and Organisation Intersex International Europe.

This report was made possible by the generous contributions of more than 350 lawyers, academics, civil society representatives, and advocates on sexual orientation, gender identity and expression, and sex characteristics (SOGIESC) issues in 64 countries. Appendix C provides the names of local experts who wish to be acknowledged.

The team appreciates the guidance provided by former World Bank Social Sustainability and Inclusion Global Practice (SSI GP) Director, Louise Cord; SSI GP Director, Robin Mearns; SSI GP Manager, Nikolas Myint; and Director for Strategy and Operations of the Sustainable Development Practice Group, Renaud Seligmann.

Finally, the team offers special thanks to the Canadian government/Global Affairs Canada for their support of this research and to the Canadian government's ongoing support to the World Bank's SOGIESC inclusion work.

Executive Summary

The World Bank Group is committed to protecting disadvantaged and vulnerable individuals and groups, including sexual and gender minorities, to ensure that they can access the benefits of development. Discrimination against sexual and gender minorities has a significant impact on their well-being, development outcomes, and ability to participate in economic opportunities. Ensuring their social and economic inclusion requires an inclusive legal and policy environment. Documenting and understanding the discriminatory laws and policies that contribute to social and economic exclusion are vital first steps toward promoting inclusive development. Gathering data on the experiences of sexual and gender minorities is critical to understanding the influence of stigma and discrimination on development outcomes.

Equality of Opportunity for Sexual and Gender Minorities 2024 (EQOSOGI) examines laws, regulations, and policies to identify provisions at the root of discriminatory practices and barriers encountered by sexual and gender minorities because of their sexual orientation, gender identity and expression, and sex characteristics (SOGIESC). This second edition of the EQOSOGI report expands its coverage from 16 to 64 countries (table ES.1).

The data, collected via questionnaires answered by local experts, cover a diverse set of countries representing various geographies, income levels, and legal traditions. The methodology used to calculate the scores in the EQOSOGI data set consists of a comprehensive analysis of the regulatory environment in each country, focusing on SOGIESC-specific laws, regulations, and policies. The scores are based on the presence or absence of specific legal, regulatory, and policy frameworks across six indicator sets: Decriminalization, Access to Education, Access to Labor Markets, Access to Services and Social Protection, Civil and Political Inclusion, and Protection from Hate Crimes. The report incorporates data disaggregation across three groups: sexual

TABLE ES.1

EQOSOGI 2024 coverage, by region

Region	Number of countries	Countries
East Asia and Pacific	10	Cambodia, China, Fiji, Indonesia, Mongolia, Papua New Guinea; Philippines, Thailand, Timor-Leste, Viet Nam
Europe and Central Asia	7	Armenia, Georgia, Kosovo, Kyrgyz Republic, Serbia, Türkiye, Ukraine
Latin America and the Caribbean	11	Argentina, Brazil, Chile, Costa Rica, Ecuador, Guyana, Haiti; Honduras, Jamaica, Mexico, Uruguay
Middle East and North Africa	8	Algeria; Djibouti; Egypt, Arab Rep.; Iraq; Jordan; Lebanon; Morocco; Tunisia
OECD high income	9	Canada; France; Germany; Israel; Japan; Korea, Rep.; New Zealand; Norway; Spain
South Asia	6	Bangladesh, Bhutan, India, Nepal, Pakistan, Sri Lanka
Sub-Saharan Africa	13	Cameroon, Côte d'Ivoire, Ethiopia, Ghana, Guinea-Bissau, Kenya; Mauritius, Mozambique, Nigeria, South Africa, Sudan, Tanzania; Zimbabwe

Source: World Bank, Equality of Opportunity for Sexual and Gender Minorities (EQOSOGI) data set, https://bit.ly/EQOSOGI2024_Online_Appendix.
Note: EQOSOGI = Equality of Opportunity for Sexual and Gender Minorities; OECD = Organisation for Economic Co-operation and Development.

orientation (lesbian, gay, and bisexual), gender identity (transgender) and expression, and sex characteristics (intersex).

The research also presents empirical findings on the association between EQOSOGI data and development outcomes, focusing on wealth, human capital, voice and accountability, income inequality, and legal frameworks. Wealthier countries tend to be more inclusive of sexual and gender minorities across all six indicator sets, with a statistically significant positive correlation between per capita real gross domestic product and overall EQOSOGI scores. The consistency of this pattern across all indicator sets suggests that economic prosperity is associated with greater inclusion of sexual and gender minorities. Higher levels of human capital and citizens' voice and accountability are also correlated with more inclusive environments for sexual and gender minorities; with statistically significant and positive correlations between EQOSOGI scores and the World Bank's Human Capital Index and Worldwide Governance Indicator estimates.

These correlations do not imply causality or indicate the direction of the relationship between development outcomes and EQOSOGI scores. The findings here are purely illustrative of the connections among education and skills, voice and accountability, and the environments supportive of sexual and gender minorities. This correlation is consistent across all indicator sets among the lesbian, gay, and bisexual; transgender; and intersex groups.

Findings by indicator set

The study finds that most of the 64 countries surveyed do not have legal and regulatory frameworks supportive of sexual and gender minority equality. Almost 55 percent of the countries in the sample (35 of 64) show a low presence of legal, regulatory, and policy frameworks favoring equality of opportunity for sexual and gender minorities. Over 40 percent of countries (26) exhibit a moderate presence of such legal, regulatory, and policy frameworks. Only 3 countries have a high presence of supportive regulatory frameworks: Canada, France, and Spain.

Decriminalization. Despite some progress, of the 64 countries measured by the EQOSOGI data set, 22 (34 percent) criminalize persons on the basis of their sexual orientation, or criminalize same-sex sexual activities, or both. Eight countries criminalize gender expression and identity, and 2 of these countries criminalize gender expression through laws against "cross-dressing." None of the 64 countries analyzed criminalizes intersex persons.

Overall, then, about 1.3 billion people live in countries (in the EQOSOGI sample) that criminalize SOGIESC-related behavior or expression. Such criminalization inhibits economic development by impeding the participation of sexual and gender minorities in their communities and limiting their contributions to society. Decriminalization not only reduces violence against sexual and gender minorities but also fosters economic development through improved access to education, health services, and employment opportunities. And it helps to create cohesive and resilient societies.

Access to Education. Students who are or are perceived to be sexual and gender minorities face higher rates of discrimination, bullying, and violence in school settings, grounded in the stigma surrounding sexual and gender diversity. Discrimination in educational settings often leads to lower educational attainment and limited opportunities for future economic success. This report finds, however, that only 31 percent of the analyzed countries (20) explicitly prohibit discrimination in educational settings on one or more SOGIESC grounds. Only 7 countries prohibit SOGIESC-based bullying, cyberbullying, and harassment in educational settings by law, and even fewer (4) prescribe SOGIESC-inclusive textbooks and curricula.

Access to Labor Markets. This report provides insights into antidiscrimination legislation and mechanisms for reporting and investigating complaints of workplace discrimination based on SOGIESC. Equal opportunity and nondiscrimination in employment are essential prerequisites for building human capital and strengthening productivity and economic growth. The research finds that 44 percent of the analyzed countries (28) prohibit discrimination in employment on one or more SOGIESC grounds, and 34 percent of countries (22) have established mechanisms for reporting and investigating complaints about labor market discrimination based on one or more SOGIESC grounds:

Access to Services and Social Protection. The analysis sheds light on laws and policies that restrict the ability of sexual and gender minorities to obtain services, often rooted in discrimination and stigma. This difficulty can exacerbate disparities in access to health care, housing, and social protection and lead to further marginalization. Only 9 of the 64 analyzed countries—Canada, Fiji, France, Germany, the Republic of Korea, Kosovo, Mauritius, Mexico, and South Africa—explicitly provide legal protection against discrimination based on sexual orientation across all three domains of services assessed by the EQOSOGI study (health care, housing, and social protection). Forty-two countries do not provide any legal protection to sexual and gender minorities in access to services. Data on the number and lived experiences of sexual and gender minorities are critical for designing inclusive laws and policies, yet only 15 percent of countries assessed by the EQOSOGI report (10) include data on sexual and gender minorities in their national census. The report also highlights the important role that SOGIESC-related civil society organizations (CSOs) play in providing access to services. Such organizations, however, are not allowed legally to register or operate in 15 of the 64 assessed countries.

Personal identification systems are vital to enabling equal access to socioeconomic opportunities, yet transgender and gender-diverse people are excluded when the law does not allow them to update their gender marker and name on official documents. Of the 64 countries analyzed, 27 allow an individual to obtain a new identification card or passport after gender reassignment, but only 14 of them allow legal gender recognition on a self-identification basis, which cuts down on administrative hurdles for gender minorities when accessing documents and services. Laws and regulations that allow for only binary options of "male" or "female" during the birth registration process severely affect intersex children, who may experience challenges throughout their lives when their gender identity differs from the sex assigned at birth that appears in official documents. Only 7 of the 64 countries assessed—Canada, Germany, Kenya, Mauritius, Nepal, New Zealand, and Spain—allow the birth registration of intersex children without a specific gender or as intersex.

Civil and Political Inclusion. The report reviews various mechanisms that enable the civil and political inclusion of sexual and gender minorities, which is critically linked to social sustainability because it ensures that all members of society have a voice in decision-making processes, feel a sense of belonging, and can actively cooperate and participate in the economy. Only 19 of the analyzed countries have national elected representatives, cabinet members, or supreme court justices who openly self-identify as a sexual or gender minority. Policies are an important tool for advancing the implementation of laws on the inclusion of sexual and gender minorities. Of the 64 countries analyzed, 17 have adopted national action plans to promote inclusion of sexual and gender minorities.

Other findings in this indicator set reveal that same-sex marriages or civil partnerships are recognized by 22 percent of the analyzed countries (14), with most of them also legally recognizing such marriages or partnerships formed in other countries. Eight of the 64 countries have enacted laws or regulations to prohibit "conversion therapy" practices, whereas 9 countries still classify being transgender as a mental disorder. Only 7 countries—Argentina, China, France, Germany, Israel, Spain, and Uruguay—prohibit irreversible surgeries on intersex children.

Protection from Hate Crimes. The analysis highlights the lack of legal frameworks in place to deter and prosecute hate crimes based on SOGIESC. It also emphasizes the lack of mechanisms to monitor and report data on SOGIESC-based hate crimes and the lack of mandatory training of law enforcement authorities. Insufficient reporting and lack of support for hate crime victims hinder understanding of the prevalence and nature of these crimes, limiting efforts to inform legal and policy reforms. Of the 64 countries analyzed, 21 explicitly criminalize hate crimes motivated by the victim's sexual orientation, and 17 criminalize crimes motivated by the victim's gender identity or expression. Hate crimes against intersex persons are not explicitly addressed in the current legislation in any of the 64 countries analyzed.

In addition, penalties for hate crimes targeting sexual and gender minorities are often not equivalent to those for hate crimes targeting other protected characteristics. The lack of legal protection from hate crimes exposes sexual and gender minorities to violence, discrimination, harassment, isolation, and social stigma. Such marginalization can exacerbate poverty among affected populations because it excludes them from development initiatives and limits their opportunities to contribute to the economy.

Groups

The EQOSOGI data highlight varying degrees of protection for three groups: (1) lesbian, gay, and bisexual; (2) transgender; and (3) intersex. Intersex people experience notably less regulatory support than lesbian, gay, and bisexual and transgender people, with no countries offering comprehensive legal frameworks for their protection.

Efforts to develop inclusive legal and regulatory frameworks for sexual and gender minorities vary across country income groups and regions. Despite strong decriminalization efforts in some regions and country income groups, even those countries show consistent weaknesses in the Access to Education, Access to Labor Markets, and Protection from Hate Crimes indicator sets (figure ES.1).

FIGURE ES.1

Distribution of EQOSOGI 2024 scores, by indicator set and region

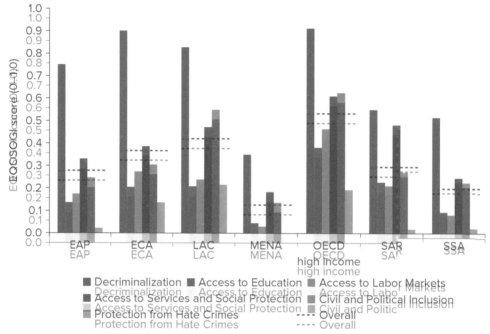

Source: World Bank, Equality of Opportunity for Sexual and Gender Minorities (EQOSOGI) data set; https://bit.ly/EQOSOGI2024_Online_Appendix.
Note: The maximum potential score per indicator set is 1, and a higher score indicates greater equality of opportunity. EAP = East Asia and Pacific; ECA = Europe and Central Asia; EQOSOGI = Equality of Opportunity for Sexual and Gender Minorities; LAC = Latin America and the Caribbean; MENA = Middle East and North Africa; OECD = Organisation for Economic Co-operation and Development; SAR = South Asia; SSA = Sub-Saharan Africa. OECD high-income countries are Canada, France, Germany, Israel, Japan, the Republic of Korea, New Zealand, Norway, and Spain.

Areas for policy engagement

The report highlights several areas for policy engagement to advance the inclusion of sexual and gender minorities:

- **Improve data collection and analysis.** Better data collection is needed on the population numbers and lived experiences of sexual and gender minorities to inform policy making and monitor progress toward inclusion, while guaranteeing the safety, privacy, and self-identification of sexual and gender minorities.

Executive Summary

- **Repeal criminalizing laws.** Countries should repeal laws that criminalize same-sex activities between consenting adults and other laws that discriminate against sexual and gender minorities. Such laws include those that consider being a sexual or gender minority a mental or physical disorder and those that criminalize "cross-dressing."

- **Ensure legal gender recognition.** Transgender and intersex individuals should have the right to legal gender recognition based on self-identification without the need for medical interventions or lengthy administrative or judicial processes.

- **Adopt laws to protect against violence and hate crimes.** Countries should enact legislation that combats SOGIESC-based violence and hate crimes, as well as harmful practices such as "conversion therapies" and irreversible, nonemergency medical surgeries on intersex children.

- **Enact inclusive legal frameworks.** Countries should adopt legal and regulatory frameworks that protect sexual and gender minorities from discrimination in various sectors, guaranteeing their equal access to education, employment, health care, housing, and social protection.

- **Ensure freedom of association for sexual and gender minorities.** Countries should repeal laws and regulations that restrict freedom of association for sexual and gender minorities and abolish laws and policies that hamper the effective operations of SOGIESC-related CSOs to foster inclusive development efforts.

Abbreviations

CSO	civil society organization
EQOSOGI	Equality of Opportunity for Sexual and Gender Minorities
GDP	gross domestic product
ICD	International Classification of Diseases
ID	identification
IPC	Indian Penal Code
LGB	lesbian, gay, and bisexual
LGBTI	lesbian, gay, bisexual, transgender, and intersex
NHRI	national human rights institution
OECD	Organisation for Economic Co-operation and Development
SOGI	Sexual Orientation and Gender Identity
SOGIESC	sexual orientation, gender identity and expression, and sex characteristics
WorLorPor committee	Committee on Determination of Unfair Gender Discrimination (Thailand)

CHAPTER 1

The EQOSOGI data set and global findings: An introduction

What does EQOSOGI measure and why?

At the core of the World Bank's mandate is a commitment to protect those who are most vulnerable or disadvantaged so that everyone—regardless of age, gender, race, ethnicity, religion, disability, social status, civic status, health status, sexual orientation, gender identity, economic disadvantages, indigenous status, or dependence on unique natural resources—can access the benefits of development (World Bank 2021).

The lives of sexual and gender minorities are marred by various intersecting discriminatory practices, thereby adversely affecting their overall well-being and their ability to participate fully and effectively in economic opportunity. These restrictions not only affect the lives of lesbian, gay, bisexual, transgender, and intersex (LGBTI) people worldwide but also limit countries' socioeconomic advancement. The cumulative effects of stigma, discrimination, and exclusion result in poor economic and human development outcomes (Badgett et al. 2014; Badgett, Waaldijk, and van der Meulen Rodgers 2019; Cortez, Arzinos, and De la Medina Soto 2021).

Nondiscrimination is at the core of the World Bank's work. For example, the Bank's Environmental and Social Framework recognizes that social inclusion and sustainable development are intertwined. That framework seeks to ensure that disadvantaged or vulnerable individuals or groups are not discriminated against in World Bank–financed projects, and that borrowers adopt differentiated measures so that such individuals and groups can take part in the opportunities resulting from these projects. Elaborating on this requirement, the World Bank Directive on Addressing Risks and Impacts on Disadvantaged or Vulnerable Individuals or Groups directs World Bank

---

A reproducibility package is available for this book in the Reproducible Research Repository at https://reproducibility.worldbank.org/index.php/catalog/182.

staff to conduct due diligence to ascertain whether sexual and gender minorities are at risk of discrimination in World Bank–financed projects and whether adequate mitigation measures have been put in place.

Recognizing such discrimination and the structural and systemic exclusion experienced by sexual and gender minorities is critical to formulating interventions to enhance the socioeconomic inclusion of LGBTI people. Although slowly emerging, the global efforts to gather data on the experiences of sexual and gender minorities remain limited (chapter 3), resulting in a paucity of data illustrating the influence of stigma, discrimination, and exclusion on development outcomes at the population level. Documenting and understanding the discriminatory laws and policies that contribute to social and economic exclusion constitute a vital first step toward promoting inclusive development.

Equality of Opportunity for Sexual and Gender Minorities (EQOSOGI) examines the state of laws, regulations, and policies to identify provisions at the root of discriminatory practices and barriers encountered by sexual and gender minorities. This second edition of EQOSOGI builds on the World Bank's ongoing efforts to monitor the regulatory barriers hindering the inclusion of certain groups in economic and human development efforts and to build strong evidence on these outcomes to support legal and policy reforms (World Bank 2024a). Inclusive legal frameworks are the starting point for fulfilling the World Bank's mission to end extreme poverty and boost prosperity on a livable planet (box 1.1).

This second edition of the EQOSOGI report starts from the premise (as elaborated in the literature review in chapter 3) that discriminatory laws and regulatory obstacles hinder the access of sexual and gender minorities to services and opportunities in education, labor markets, and economic participation. These barriers, which impede human development and economic opportunities, are also evident in the systemic challenges faced by sexual and gender minorities in forming organizations, expressing identities, participating in politics, changing gender markers in official documents, entering civil partnerships or marriages, adopting children, and seeking asylum.

Sexual and gender minorities are victims of hate crimes and hate speech in many countries, with instances of criminalization exacerbating their plight. Widespread discrimination and persecution persist, particularly in countries where same-sex activities are illegal or criminalized. When these injustices become ingrained in legal frameworks, the potential for sexual and gender minorities to actively participate in the development process becomes constrained, thereby hindering overall economic growth.

BOX 1.1 How does the World Bank integrate SOGIESC inclusion in its work?

There is growing recognition of the importance of embedding sexual orientation, gender identity and expression, and sex characteristics (SOGIESC) inclusion in international development efforts. Since 2015, the World Bank has grounded SOGIESC inclusion in its commitments to gender equality, social inclusion, and nondiscrimination; and that year saw the creation of an internal World Bank–wide Sexual Orientation and Gender Identity (SOGI) Task Force, made up of representatives of many Global Practices and other World Bank units. The SOGI Task Force remains active and is currently chaired by the World Bank's Chief Environmental and Social Officer.

The World Bank's Social Sustainability and Inclusion Global Practice has given definition to SOGIESC inclusion as part of social inclusion, which is the process of improving the ability, opportunity, and dignity of those disadvantaged on the basis of their identity to take part in society. It is part of the World Bank's broader goal of building social sustainability into development, as laid out in the World Bank's Social Sustainability and Inclusion Strategy (Barron et al. 2023).

The World Bank's Environmental and Social Framework, particularly through its Directive on Disadvantaged or Vulnerable Individuals or Groups, also anchors SOGI inclusion within the principle of nondiscrimination.

The new World Bank Group Gender Strategy 2024–2030 places a greater emphasis on SOGIESC inclusion (World Bank 2024b). The strategy explicitly encompasses sexual and gender minorities in each of its pillars of work, and it incorporates SOGIESC into its gender tag corporate tracking.

Finally, the World Bank's SOGI Global Advisor and team provide thought leadership and technical assistance to World Bank staff and government borrowers through World Bank–financed projects.

This study builds on and complements the methodology and findings of the EQOSOGI pilot project, published in 2021. The pilot study gathered data in 16 countries on the legal frameworks affecting sexual and gender minorities (Cortez, Arzinos, and De la Medina Soto 2021). This second edition expands the coverage to 64 countries. Although this edition maintains the original six indicator sets—Decriminalization, Access to Education, Access to Labor Markets, Access to Services and Social Protection, Civil and Political Inclusion, and Protection from Hate Crimes—it updates and refines the methodology for the questions measured (appendixes A and B). This expanded edition for the first time incorporates data disaggregation across three groups, providing separate scores for (1) sexual orientation, (2) gender identity and expression, and (3) sex characteristics.

This report provides a comprehensive overview of the laws and policies that either enable or undermine inclusion or that offer protective measures for sexual and gender minorities. The report identifies the elements of the legal and policy frameworks that countries can strengthen to ensure wider inclusion (this chapter). It also includes a comprehensive overview of laws that discriminate on the basis of sexual orientation, gender identity and expression, and sex characteristics (SOGIESC) (chapter 2). Finally, this expanded edition also explores the relationship between SOGIESC-inclusive laws and policies and development outcomes such as economic growth and social sustainability (chapter 3).

Data collection and analysis

EQOSOGI data are based on an analysis of laws and policies obtained from question-naires completed (pro bono) by lawyers, academics, and civil society representatives and advocates on SOGIESC issues in countries included in the sample. The question-naires aim to collect and verify the laws, regulations, and policies measured.[1]

The study covers 64 countries (map 1.1). These countries are representative of several key characteristics: (1) diverse geographies representing all World Bank regions[2] (table 1.1); (2) income levels representing low-income, lower-middle-income, upper-middle-income, and high-income countries; (3) various legal traditions; and (4) varying levels of inclusiveness of sexual and gender minorities (from less inclusive to more inclusive), thereby ensuring a diverse yet holistic picture of these issues.

The report updates data on the 16 countries covered by the pilot EQOSOGI report: Bangladesh, Canada, Costa Rica, India, Indonesia, Jamaica, Japan, Kosovo, Lebanon, Mexico, Mozambique, Nigeria, South Africa, Tunisia, Ukraine, and Uruguay. The World Bank team collected data for 31 additional countries. The Asian Development Bank, applying the established World Bank data collection protocols, led the data collec-tion for 17 countries: Armenia, Bhutan, Cambodia, China, Fiji, Georgia, the Republic of Korea, the Kyrgyz Republic, Mongolia, Nepal, New Zealand, Papua New Guinea, the Philippines, Sri Lanka, Thailand, Timor-Leste, and Viet Nam. The World Bank guided the Asian Development Bank's data analysis by sharing questionnaires and the EQOSOGI methodology, and by performing quality control (ADB 2024).

Data collection took place from February 15 to June 1, 2023, by means of a standard-ized expert questionnaire administered to lawyers, academics, civil society repre-sentatives, and advocates on SOGIESC issues. Overall, more than 400 local experts

The EQOSOGI data set and global findings: An introduction

MAP 1.1

EQOSOGI 2024 coverage, pilot and expansion countries
EQOSOGI 2024 coverage, pilot and expansion countries

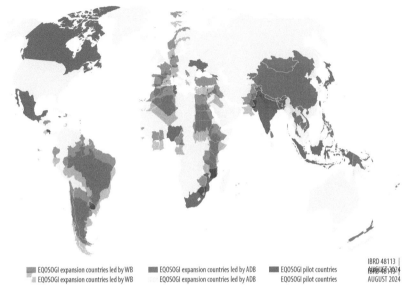

■ EQOSOGI expansion countries led by WB ■ EQOSOGI expansion countries led by ADB ■ EQOSOGI pilot countries

IBRD 48113 |
AUGUST 2024

Source: World Bank, Equality of Opportunity for Sexual and Gender Minorities (EQOSOGI) data set, https://bit.ly/EQOSOGI2024_Online_Appendix.

Note: ADB = Asian Development Bank; WB = World Bank.

TABLE 1.1

EQOSOGI 2024 coverage, by region

Region	Number of countries	Countries
East Asia and Pacific	10	Cambodia, China, Fiji, Indonesia, Mongolia, Papua New Guinea, Philippines, Thailand, Timor-Leste, Viet Nam
Europe and Central Asia	7	Armenia, Georgia, Kosovo, Kyrgyz Republic, Serbia, Türkiye, Ukraine
Latin America and the Caribbean	11	Argentina, Brazil, Chile, Costa Rica, Ecuador, Guyana, Haiti, Honduras, Jamaica, Mexico, Uruguay
Middle East and North Africa	8	Algeria; Djibouti; Egypt, Arab Rep.; Iraq; Jordan; Lebanon; Morocco; Tunisia
OECD high income	9	Canada; France; Germany; Israel; Japan; Korea, Rep.; New Zealand; Norway; Spain
South Asia	6	Bangladesh, Bhutan, India, Nepal, Pakistan, Sri Lanka
Sub-Saharan Africa	13	Cameroon, Côte d'Ivoire, Ethiopia, Ghana, Guinea-Bissau, Kenya, Mauritius, Mozambique, Nigeria, South Africa, Sudan, Tanzania, Zimbabwe

Source: World Bank, Equality of Opportunity for Sexual and Gender Minorities (EQOSOGI) data set, https://bit.ly/EQOSOGI2024_Online_Appendix.

Note: EQOSOGI = Equality of Opportunity for Sexual and Gender Minorities; OECD = Organisation for Economic Co-operation and Development.

contributed to the data collection by responding to the standardized questionnaire (refer to appendix C for a list of those experts). The role of these local expert respondents is to provide legal sources and complement the knowledge of the World Bank team.

The EQOSOGI team has analysts with experience in the topics measured by the study, including political scientists, social scientists, economists, and lawyers familiar with different legal systems. These analysts verified questionnaire responses by assessing the text of all legal sources provided by expert respondents and supplemented the analysis with publicly available data. They analyzed the information provided by country-based contributors and cross-checked the responses against relevant laws and regulations. For example, the EQOSOGI team examined the relevant criminal codes for each country assessed by the study to determine whether the country criminalizes same-sex relations between consenting adults.

The EQOSOGI second edition builds on questions grouped into the six sets of indicators constructed for the pilot edition in 2021 in consultations with global experts on SOGIESC inclusion. For consistency purposes, where relevant, EQOSOGI adopted indicator language from "A Set of Proposed Indicators for the LGBTI Inclusion Index" (Badgett and Sell 2018). This index was developed under the leadership of the World Bank and the United Nations Development Programme with civil society organizations (CSOs) and other stakeholders; these indicators are intended to populate the LGBTI Inclusion Index, a United Nations Development Programme initiative.

The following six sets of indicators assess laws and regulations that affect sexual and gender minorities' socioeconomic inclusion:

1. *Decriminalization* examines the criminalization of same-sex behavior and expression related to gender identity and sex characteristics.
2. *Access to Education* assesses equal access to public education of a consistent quality.
3. *Access to Labor Markets* identifies legislation that protects sexual and gender minorities from discrimination in employment.
4. *Access to Services and Social Protection* examines the ability of sexual and gender minorities to equally access services and social protection, including health care services, and the ability of CSOs to provide such services. It also assesses the enabling environment for trans people to access legal gender recognition.
5. *Civil and Political Inclusion* examines the degree of participation by sexual and gender minorities, including equal rights to marriage and family, the prohibition

of "conversion therapy" practices, and protections from nonemergency surgeries for intersex children.

6. *Protection from Hate Crimes* identifies laws and mechanisms that criminalize SOGIESC-based hate crimes and provide protection for victims.

Construction of the EQOSOGI data set and scores

EQOSOGI scores were constructed in three steps:

1. All qualitative legal responses to the 138 questions were coded as a binary qualitative answer (Yes/No) and transformed into binary quantitative responses (0/1) in which 1 denotes equality of opportunity for the specific minority group (for example, lesbian, gay, and bisexual [LGB]; transgender; or intersex people) in the corresponding question and 0 denotes no equality of opportunity.

2. Quality control of the computed binary responses was conducted, especially to review the consistency of the computed binary responses and the variability and presence of outliers in the distribution of each binary response.

3. Computation of the overall EQOSOGI country scores and SOGIESC group scores was carried out using a two-step averaging process. Initially, indicator set scores were calculated by averaging all binary responses within each of the six indicator sets. Subsequently, to determine the EQOSOGI country scores or group scores, an average of the six indicator set scores was computed. This two-step averaging process ensured equal weighting within and between indicator sets.[3] Indicator set and overall scores were calculated for each country, for each region, for the whole sample of 64 countries, for all income groups, and for the three SOGIESC groups. All results are shown in tables 1.2 and 1.3 and in figures 1.1 to 1.5 in the "Global findings" section.

The values of the scores range from 0 to 1. A country receiving an EQOSOGI score of 0 does not have legal, regulatory, and policy frameworks in favor of equality of opportunity for sexual and gender minorities. An economy receiving an EQOSOGI score of 1 has legal, regulatory, and policy frameworks for all six indicator sets, thereby favoring equality of opportunity for sexual and gender minorities. For the EQOSOGI scores, the distribution over 64 countries is sorted into the following categories of presence of regulatory frameworks: low (0–0.29), moderate (0.30–0.60), and high (0.61–1). Refer to appendix B for a detailed discussion of the scope of the scoring methodology. This categorization has been adopted for widely known development metrics such as the Human Development Index and the CIVICUS monitor score, which divide the possible range of values of their scores from very low to very high.

Strengths and limitations of the methodology

The collected data refer predominantly to the formal legal and regulatory environment (de jure) in the analyzed countries and, in some instances, to government policies on the treatment of sexual and gender minorities. Policies emanating from different government entities are used to measure, for example, the existence of national action plans on SOGIESC; the prohibition of SOGIESC-based bullying, cyberbullying, and harassment in educational settings; the integration of SOGIESC-inclusive sexuality education in curricula; the regulation of workplace attire and school dress codes; the existence of laws prohibiting sexual and gender minorities or those who engage in same-sex behaviors from donating blood; and the training of professionals to recognize and identify SOGIESC-based hate crimes. The practice or implementation of the law (de facto) is covered only tangentially by identifying enforcement mechanisms that serve as proxies of implementation such as enforcing criminal provisions related to "indecent acts" and "public morals" to target same-sex sexual activities and diverse gender identities and expressions, as well as mechanisms for reporting and monitoring hate crimes. The questionnaire also asks about the number of national elected representatives, cabinet members, and supreme court justices who openly self-identify as a sexual or gender minority.

Measuring codified laws allows direct comparisons of countries, but it also presents some limitations. For example, the study is limited to the formal economy and so cannot capture the experiences of sexual and gender minorities in the informal economy. Yet those experiences may contribute to barriers to their socioeconomic development. Customary and religious or personal laws are not captured because of their often-uncodified status and the resulting difficulties in defining the rules. Gaps in the implementation of the laws are not assessed either. Furthermore, only legislation applicable to the largest business city in federal countries is analyzed. The data may therefore not be representative of areas where subnational law applies. This approach helps ensure that EQOSOGI indicators are comparable across countries and actionable, the law being what policy makers can change. International human rights law is also outside the scope of the study, which focuses only on national laws. Although international conventions—including the International Covenant on Economic, Social and Cultural Rights; the International Covenant on Civil and Political Rights; and the Convention on the Elimination of All Forms of Discrimination against Women—seek to ensure equality before the law and protection from violence, the report does not review these conventions or their application in the 64 countries in this study.

Furthermore, to inspire discourse on legal and policy reforms, the EQOSOGI report presents select examples of positive legal, regulatory, and policy developments from countries outside the study sample (refer to box 2.2 in chapter 2). However, these examples do not contribute to the comparative legal and empirical analysis presented in the report.

Data in the EQOSOGI data set are current as of June 1, 2023. The analysis does not consider laws, regulations, and policies enacted after this date.

Global findings

Across the 64 countries, the average overall score is 0.31, indicating a low to moderate presence of regulatory frameworks favoring equality of opportunities for sexual and gender minorities (figure 1.1). More than half of the countries in the sample (35 out of 64, or 54.7 percent) indicate a low presence of regulatory frameworks favoring equality of opportunity for sexual and gender minorities, whereas 26 countries (40.6 percent) exhibit a moderate presence of regulatory frameworks. Only three countries—Canada, France, and Spain—have a high presence of regulatory frameworks. Table 1.2 shows the scores of all countries.

The analysis by indicator set in figure 1.1 reveals that countries still need to advance in all indicator sets. Although Decriminalization has a high average score, 0.69, many countries continue to criminalize SOGIESC-related behavior and acts, thereby fundamentally undermining socioeconomic participation for sexual and gender minorities. Criminalization of SOGIESC creates structural barriers that prevent sexual and gender minorities from exercising their basic freedoms and rights and bar them from contributing to human and economic development. Criminalization also fuels stigma, and consequently it pushes sexual and gender minorities to the margins of society and puts them at greater risk of violence and abuse. Although legal progress toward decriminalization is under way in East Asia and Pacific, Europe, Latin America and the Caribbean, South Asia, and Sub-Saharan Africa, many countries (more than 30 percent of those in the EQOSOGI data set) continue to criminalize same-sex activity and/or gender expression and identity (refer to chapter 2).

Protection from Hate Crimes exhibits the lowest average score (0.09), highlighting the pressing need for improvement. Access to Education, Access to Labor Markets, Access to Services and Social Protection, and Civil and Political Inclusion produce

FIGURE 1.1

Distribution of EQOSOGI 2024 scores, overall and by indicator set

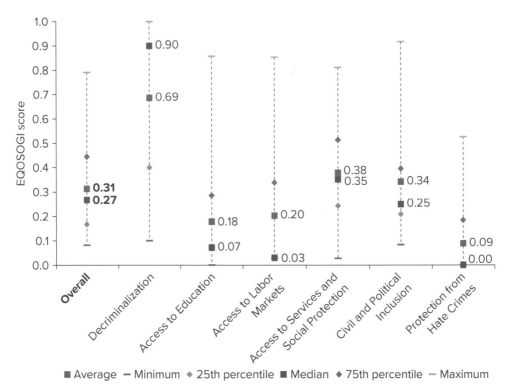

■ Average ― Minimum ◆ 25th percentile ■ Median ◆ 75th percentile ― Maximum

Source: World Bank, Equality of Opportunity for Sexual and Gender Minorities (EQOSOGI) data set, https://bit.ly/EQOSOGI2024_Online_Appendix.

Note: For Decriminalization, the median and 75th percentile scores match. For Access to Education, Access to Labor Markets, and Protection from Hate Crimes, the median and 25th percentile scores match.

low to moderate average scores, between 0.18 and 0.38 (figure 1.1). Countries are moving toward more inclusive education systems and labor markets—at least 31 percent of the analyzed countries have enacted laws and regulations to prohibit discrimination in the education sector on one or more grounds of SOGIESC, and at least 40 percent of the analyzed countries have enacted laws and regulations to prohibit employment-related discrimination on one or more grounds of SOGIESC (refer to chapter 2).

TABLE 1.2

EQOSOGI scores by country, overall and by indicator set

Country	Overall	Decrimi-nalization	Access to Education	Access to Labor Markets	Access to Services and Social Protection	Civil and Political Inclusion	Protection from Hate Crimes
Algeria	0.11	0.30	0.07	0.03	0.14	0.13	0.00
Argentina	0.47	0.90	0.07	0.18	0.51	0.83	0.32
Armenia	0.27	0.90	0.07	0.03	0.35	0.25	0.00
Bangladesh	0.18	0.30	0.07	0.03	0.41	0.29	0.00
Bhutan	0.26	0.90	0.07	0.03	0.32	0.25	0.00
Brazil	0.54	1.00	0.36	0.32	0.57	0.67	0.32
Cambodia	0.20	0.60	0.07	0.03	0.27	0.25	0.00
Cameroon	0.14	0.40	0.07	0.03	0.19	0.13	0.00
Canada	0.71	1.00	0.57	0.65	0.81	0.92	0.32
Chile	0.53	1.00	0.36	0.38	0.49	0.75	0.21
China	0.16	0.60	0.07	0.03	0.11	0.13	0.00
Costa Rica	0.49	1.00	0.21	0.32	0.46	0.75	0.21
Côte d'Ivoire	0.19	0.70	0.07	0.03	0.19	0.13	0.00
Djibouti	0.27	0.90	0.07	0.03	0.35	0.25	0.00
Ecuador	0.59	0.90	0.64	0.59	0.59	0.54	0.26
Egypt, Arab Rep.	0.11	0.30	0.00	0.03	0.19	0.13	0.00
Ethiopia	0.10	0.30	0.07	0.03	0.05	0.13	0.00
Fiji	0.41	0.90	0.21	0.53	0.59	0.25	0.00
France	0.61	0.90	0.21	0.68	0.70	0.88	0.26
Georgia	0.43	0.90	0.36	0.24	0.38	0.33	0.37
Germany	0.54	1.00	0.43	0.35	0.59	0.71	0.16
Ghana	0.11	0.30	0.07	0.03	0.03	0.21	0.00
Guinea-Bissau	0.27	0.90	0.07	0.03	0.35	0.25	0.00
Guyana	0.17	0.30	0.07	0.03	0.35	0.25	0.00
Haiti	0.27	0.90	0.07	0.03	0.35	0.25	0.00
Honduras	0.37	0.90	0.07	0.26	0.35	0.29	0.37
India	0.52	0.60	0.79	0.65	0.68	0.29	0.11
Indonesia	0.19	0.60	0.07	0.03	0.27	0.17	0.00
Iraq	0.09	0.30	0.07	0.03	0.05	0.08	0.00
Israel	0.42	0.90	0.43	0.29	0.46	0.33	0.11
Jamaica	0.18	0.40	0.07	0.03	0.35	0.25	0.00

(continued)

EQOSOGI scores by country, overall and by indicator set *(continued)*

Country	Overall	Decrimi-nalization	Access to Education	Access to Labor Markets	Access to Services and Social Protection	Civil and Political Inclusion	Protection from Hate Crimes
Japan	0.27	0.90	0.07	0.03	0.38	0.25	0.00
Jordan	0.12	0.40	0.07	0.03	0.11	0.13	0.00
Kenya	0.19	0.40	0.07	0.03	0.41	0.25	0.00
Korea, Rep.	0.31	0.60	0.21	0.29	0.49	0.25	0.00
Kosovo	0.54	0.90	0.36	0.71	0.62	0.46	0.21
Kyrgyz Republic	0.23	0.90	0.00	0.03	0.22	0.25	0.00
Lebanon	0.08	0.10	0.07	0.03	0.16	0.13	0.00
Mauritius	0.31	0.50	0.29	0.32	0.49	0.29	0.00
Mexico	0.53	0.90	0.29	0.32	0.57	0.67	0.42
Mongolia	0.35	0.90	0.07	0.47	0.38	0.25	0.05
Morocco	0.11	0.30	0.00	0.03	0.19	0.13	0.00
Mozambique	0.31	0.90	0.07	0.09	0.35	0.25	0.21
Nepal	0.24	0.50	0.07	0.03	0.51	0.33	0.00
New Zealand	0.54	1.00	0.36	0.35	0.68	0.75	0.11
Nigeria	0.14	0.50	0.07	0.03	0.03	0.21	0.00
Norway	0.59	0.90	0.29	0.68	0.62	0.79	0.26
Pakistan	0.40	0.70	0.36	0.50	0.62	0.21	0.00
Papua New Guinea	0.19	0.60	0.07	0.03	0.19	0.25	0.00
Philippines	0.36	0.60	0.43	0.38	0.38	0.29	0.11
Serbia	0.54	0.90	0.50	0.56	0.49	0.42	0.37
South Africa	0.41	0.90	0.14	0.35	0.54	0.46	0.05
Spain	0.79	1.00	0.86	0.85	0.76	0.75	0.53
Sri Lanka	0.16	0.30	0.00	0.03	0.35	0.25	0.00
Sudan	0.10	0.20	0.07	0.03	0.19	0.13	0.00
Tanzania	0.13	0.40	0.07	0.03	0.03	0.25	0.00
Thailand	0.35	0.90	0.21	0.18	0.46	0.38	0.00
Timor-Leste	0.28	0.90	0.07	0.03	0.35	0.25	0.05
Tunisia	0.10	0.20	0.00	0.03	0.27	0.13	0.00
Türkiye	0.25	0.90	0.07	0.03	0.27	0.25	0.00
Ukraine	0.31	0.90	0.07	0.32	0.38	0.17	0.00

(continued)

The EQOSOGI data set and global findings: An introduction

TABLE 1.2

EQOSOGI scores by country, overall and by indicator set *(continued)*

Country	Overall	Decrimi-nalization	Access to Education	Access to Labor Markets	Access to Services and Social Protection	Civil and Political Inclusion	Protection from Hate Crimes
Uruguay	0.46	0.90	0.07	0.15	0.59	0.79	0.26
Viet Nam	0.26	0.90	0.07	0.03	0.29	0.25	0.00
Zimbabwe	0.17	0.30	0.07	0.03	0.35	0.25	0.00

Source: World Bank, Equality of Opportunity for Sexual and Gender Minorities (EQOSOGI) data set, https://bit.ly/EQOSOGI2024_Online_Appendix.

Note: ■ ≡ high presence of regulatory frameworks; ■ = moderate presence of regulatory frameworks; ■ ≡ low presence of regulatory frameworks.

An analysis of the three SOGIESC groups—LGB, transgender, and intersex—reveals a consistent pattern of limited regulatory support across all groups, yet with noticeable disparities that particularly disadvantage the intersex group. When one delves into the EQOSOGI scores at the group level, the results do not vary significantly from the overall aggregated scores. The average scores across the groups are 0.24 for the intersex group, indicating a low presence of regulatory frameworks, and 0.31 for the LGB group and 0.32 for the transgender group, indicating a moderate presence of regulatory frameworks (figure 1.2). This outcome underscores the need for concerted efforts to enhance protection of and support for all three groups. Nevertheless, noteworthy differences exist between the groups. In the LGB group, eight countries demonstrate a high presence of regulatory frameworks; in the transgender group, four countries show a similar level of support. In stark contrast, in the intersex group, no country reaches this level of support (table 1.3).

This disparity highlights that, although all groups need focused interventions, the intersex group's needs are more urgent, requiring substantial measures. Illustrating this finding, figure 1.3 reports the scores of LGB, transgender, and intersex groups by region. The intersex group exhibits greater inclusion in the South Asia region than in other regions. In the Middle East and North Africa, the LGB group is at a greater disadvantage than the intersex one. In Sub-Saharan Africa, average EQOSOGI scores for the LGB and intersex groups are almost identical, with both scoring lower than the transgender group. Figure 1.3 also highlights the interregional differences in the average EQOSOGI scores, with high-income Organisation for Economic Co-operation and Development (OECD) countries having the highest average score and countries in the Middle East and North Africa, the lowest average score.

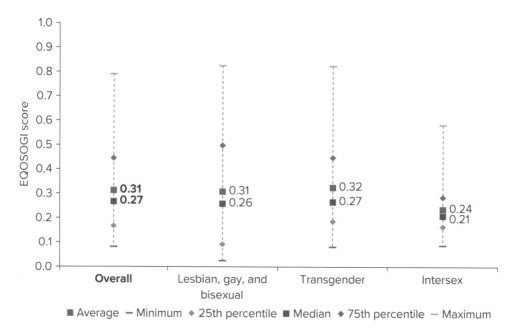

FIGURE 1.2

Distribution of EQOSOGI 2024 scores, overall and by SOGIESC group

■ Average — Minimum ◆ 25th percentile ■ Median ◆ 75th percentile — Maximum

Source: World Bank, Equality of Opportunity for Sexual and Gender Minorities (EQOSOGI) data set, https://bit.ly/EQOSOGI2024_Online_Appendix.
Note: SOGIESC = sexual orientation, gender identity and expression, and sex characteristics.

TABLE 1.3

EQOSOGI scores by country, overall and by SOGIESC group

Country	Overall	Lesbian, gay, and bisexual	Transgender	Intersex
Algeria	0.11	0.04	0.18	0.11
Argentina	0.47	0.50	0.46	0.34
Armenia	0.27	0.27	0.24	0.21
Bangladesh	0.18	0.05	0.26	0.21
Bhutan	0.26	0.24	0.25	0.20
Brazil	0.54	0.57	0.57	0.40
Cambodia	0.20	0.20	0.21	0.14
Cameroon	0.14	0.05	0.18	0.17
Canada	0.71	0.77	0.78	0.43
Chile	0.53	0.57	0.55	0.28
China	0.16	0.11	0.14	0.18

(continued)

TABLE 1.3

EQOSOGI scores by country, overall and by SOGIESC group *(continued)*

Country	Overall	Lesbian, gay, and bisexual	Transgender	Intersex
Costa Rica	0.49	0.59	0.47	0.38
Côte d'Ivoire	0.19	0.14	0.22	0.17
Djibouti	0.27	0.26	0.27	0.21
Ecuador	0.59	0.67	0.59	0.28
Egypt, Arab Rep.	0.11	0.05	0.16	0.11
Ethiopia	0.10	0.04	0.15	0.09
Fiji	0.41	0.48	0.45	0.21
France	0.61	0.71	0.66	0.33
Georgia	0.43	0.46	0.37	0.22
Germany	0.54	0.69	0.45	0.42
Ghana	0.11	0.03	0.17	0.11
Guinea-Bissau	0.27	0.26	0.27	0.21
Guyana	0.17	0.09	0.18	0.21
Haiti	0.27	0.26	0.27	0.21
Honduras	0.37	0.37	0.39	0.24
India	0.52	0.36	0.57	0.50
Indonesia	0.19	0.20	0.19	0.12
Iraq	0.09	0.03	0.14	0.10
Israel	0.42	0.52	0.35	0.26
Jamaica	0.18	0.09	0.22	0.21
Japan	0.27	0.27	0.28	0.24
Jordan	0.12	0.16	0.08	0.10
Kenya	0.19	0.09	0.22	0.23
Korea, Rep.	0.31	0.39	0.29	0.21
Kosovo	0.54	0.53	0.54	0.38
Kyrgyz Republic	0.23	0.23	0.23	0.20
Lebanon	0.08	0.04	0.08	0.10
Mauritius	0.31	0.41	0.25	0.21
Mexico	0.53	0.70	0.42	0.32
Mongolia	0.35	0.37	0.38	0.23
Morocco	0.11	0.05	0.16	0.11

(continued)

TABLE 1.3

EQOSOGI scores by country, overall and by SOGIESC group *(continued)*

Country	Overall	Lesbian, gay, and bisexual	Transgender	Intersex
Mozambique	0.31	0.32	0.29	0.21
Nepal	0.24	0.20	0.26	0.20
New Zealand	0.54	0.72	0.44	0.38
Nigeria	0.14	0.07	0.17	0.16
Norway	0.59	0.66	0.61	0.29
Pakistan	0.40	0.09	0.56	0.53
Papua New Guinea	0.19	0.11	0.24	0.19
Philippines	0.36	0.43	0.41	0.29
Serbia	0.54	0.55	0.57	0.29
South Africa	0.41	0.59	0.29	0.24
Spain	0.79	0.83	0.82	0.58
Sri Lanka	0.16	0.08	0.20	0.15
Sudan	0.10	0.05	0.14	0.11
Tanzania	0.13	0.04	0.17	0.16
Thailand	0.35	0.30	0.45	0.27
Timor-Leste	0.28	0.27	0.27	0.21
Tunisia	0.10	0.07	0.13	0.12
Türkiye	0.25	0.24	0.25	0.20
Ukraine	0.31	0.33	0.33	0.20
Uruguay	0.46	0.50	0.45	0.29
Viet Nam	0.26	0.24	0.27	0.21
Zimbabwe	0.17	0.09	0.18	0.21

Source: World Bank, Equality of Opportunity for Sexual and Gender Minorities (EQOSOGI) data set; https://bit.ly/EQOSOGI2024_Online_Appendix.

Note: ■ = high presence of regulatory frameworks; ■ = moderate presence of regulatory frameworks; □ = low presence of regulatory frameworks. SOGIESC = sexual orientation, gender identity and expression; and sex characteristics.

Legal frameworks supporting SOGIESC inclusion also vary across indicator sets and regions (figure 1.4). Like the global-level trends, Decriminalization is the strongest indicator set in every region and is especially strong in OECD high-income countries (0.91), Europe and Central Asia (0.90), Latin America and the Caribbean (0.83), and East Asia and Pacific (0.75). Next come Access to Services and Social Protection in the OECD high-income economies, Latin America and the Caribbean, South Asia, and Europe and Central Asia, and Civil and Political Inclusion in OECD high-income

FIGURE 1.3

Distribution of EQOSOGI 2024 scores, overall and by SOGIESC group and region

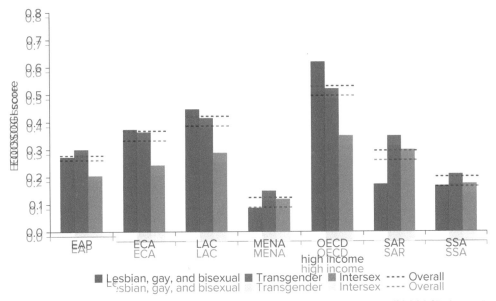

Source: World Bank; Equality of Opportunity for Sexual and Gender Minorities (EQOSOGI) data set, https://bit.ly/EQOSOGI2024_Online_Appendix.

Note: OECD high income includes Canada, France, Germany, Israel, Japan, the Republic of Korea, New Zealand, Norway, and Spain. EAP = East Asia and Pacific; ECA = Europe and Central Asia; LAC: Latin America and the Caribbean; MENA = Middle East and North Africa; OECD = Organisation for Economic Co-operation and Development; SAR = South Asia; SOGIESC = sexual orientation, gender identity and expression, and sex characteristics; SSA = Sub-Saharan Africa.

economies and Latin America and the Caribbean. Access to Education and Access to Labor Markets lag behind those three indicator sets. Finally, Protection from Hate Crimes is the weakest indicator set in every region, especially in the Middle East and North Africa (0), East Asia and Pacific (0.02), South Asia (0.02), and Sub-Saharan Africa (0.02). Even in regions with relatively high levels of inclusion as reflected in some indicator sets (such as Decriminalization), SOGIESC minorities continue to face exclusion in other indicator sets (such as Access to Education). Meanwhile, trends for the indicator sets are fairly consistent within each region. Most regions have relatively strong protections against criminalization; moderate to low protections for Access to Services and Social Protection, Civil and Political Inclusion, Access to Labor Markets, and Access to Education; and significantly lower protections for Protection from Hate Crimes.

FIGURE 1.4

Distribution of EQOSOGI 2024 scores, by indicator set and region

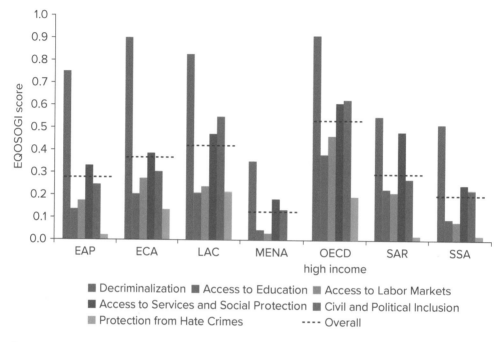

Source: World Bank, Equality of Opportunity for Sexual and Gender Minorities (EQOSOGI) data set, https://bit.ly/EQOSOGI2024_Online_Appendix.

Note: OECD high income includes Canada, France, Germany, Israel, Japan, the Republic of Korea, New Zealand, Norway, and Spain. EAP = East Asia and Pacific; ECA = Europe and Central Asia; LAC = Latin America and the Caribbean; MENA = Middle East and North Africa; OECD = Organisation for Economic Co-operation and Development; SAR = South Asia; SSA = Sub-Saharan Africa.

Similar trends appear when countries are grouped according to income status (figure 1.5). Decriminalization is the strongest indicator set across all country income groups at 0.87 in high-income countries, 0.79 in upper-middle-income countries, 0.56 in lower-middle-income countries, and 0.58 in low-income countries,[4] followed by Access to Services and Social Protection, and Civil and Political Inclusion. As in the regional groups, Access to Education and Access to Labor Markets lag behind, and Protection from Hate Crimes is the lowest indicator set for each income group. Overall, SOGIESC-based legal protections are better among high-income and upper-middle-income countries. However, countries across all income groups have significant room for improvement in several indicator sets, especially in Access to Education, Access to Labor Markets, and Protection from Hate Crimes.

FIGURE 1.5

Distribution of EQOSOGI 2024 scores, by indicator set and country income group

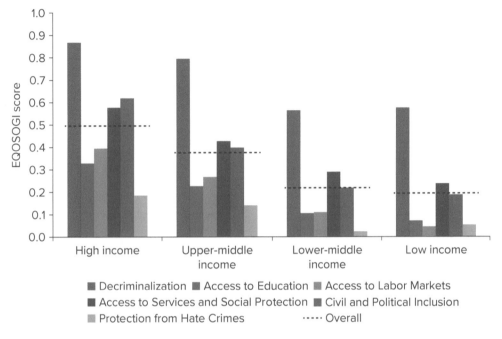

Source: World Bank, Equality of Opportunity for Sexual and Gender Minorities (EQOSOGI) data set, https://bit.ly/EQOSOGI2024_Online_Appendix.
Note: Country income classifications are based on 2022 gross national income: high income = US$13,846 or more, upper-middle income = US$4,466 to US$13,845, lower-middle income = US$1,136 to US$4,465, low-income = US$1,135 or less.

Notes

1. A minimum threshold of five fully completed questionnaires was established per country. At least five or more fully completed questionnaires were received for 58 countries; however, the team received only four completed questionnaires for Algeria, Iraq, Jordan, and Kosovo, and two fully completed surveys for Djibouti and Sudan, despite the team's efforts to recruit additional contributors in these countries. The outbreak of military hostilities in Sudan in April 2023 further hindered response efforts by significantly impeding communication and access to potential contributors within the country. The information provided in the received questionnaires in conjunction with publicly available sources was deemed sufficient to ensure data quality, accuracy, and transparency for all 64 countries covered by the study.
2. The World Bank regional classification has two variants. This report adopts the classification that groups Organisation for Economic Co-operation and Development (OECD) high-income economies into a single category, and other economies into the East Asia and Pacific, Europe and Central Asia, Latin America and the Caribbean, Middle East and North Africa, South Asia, and Sub-Saharan Africa regions. Note that the alternative classification includes North America and ignores the OECD high-income category.

3. For robustness purposes, a simple mean approach was also computed to obtain the overall score. To do so, the responses of the 138 questions were averaged across the six indicator sets. Averages per indicator set and per SOGIESC group were computed by averaging the responses of the questions within each of the six indicator sets and SOGIESC groups. The results of this approach and the two-step averaging approach were robust, showing a statistically significant rank correlation of 0.98 at the 1 percent significance level.

4. Income classifications are based on 2022 gross national income: high income ≡ US$13,846 or more, upper-middle income = US$4,466 to US$13,845, lower-middle income ≡ US$1,136 to US$4,465, low income = US$1,135 or less. Refer also to World Bank, "World Bank Country and Lending Groups," https://datahelpdesk.worldbank.org/knowledgebase/articles/906519 -world-bank-country-and-lending-groups.

References

ADB (Asian Development Bank). 2024. *The Assessment of the Legal Status of Sexual and Gender Minorities in 17 Countries in Asia and the Pacific*. Manila: Asian Development Bank.

Badgett, M. V. L., S. Nezhad, K. Waaldijk, and Y. van der Meulen Rodgers. 2014. "The Relationship between LGBT Inclusion and Economic Development: An Analysis of Emerging Economies." Williams Institute, UCLA School of Law, University of California, Los Angeles. https:// williamsinstitute.law.ucla.edu/wp-content/uploads/lgbt-inclusion-and-development -november-2014.pdf.

Badgett, M. V. L., and R. Sell. 2018. "A Set of Proposed Indicators for the LGBTI Inclusion Index." United Nations Development Programme, New York. https://www.undp.org/sites/g/files /zskgke326/files/publications/ENGLISH_LGBTI_index_march2019.pdf.

Badgett, M. V. L., K. Waaldijk, and Y. van der Meulen Rodgers. 2019. "The Relationship between LGBT Inclusion and Economic Development: Macro-Level Evidence." *World Development* 120: 1–14.

Barron, P., L. Cord, J. Cuesta, S. A. Espinoza, G. Larson, and M. Woolcock. 2023. *Social Sustainability in Development: Meeting the Challenges of the 21st Century. New Frontiers of Social Policy*. Washington, DC: World Bank.

Cortez, C., J. Arzinos, and C. De la Medina Soto. 2021. *Equality of Opportunity for Sexual and Gender Minorities*. Washington, DC: World Bank. http://hdl.handle.net/10986/36288.

World Bank. 2021. *The Human Capital Index: Human Capital in the Time of COVID-19*. Washington, DC: World Bank. https://openknowledge.worldbank.org/entities/publication /93f8fbc6-4513-58e7-82ec-af4636380319.

World Bank. 2024a. *Women, Business and the Law 2024*. Washington, DC: World Bank.

World Bank. 2024b. *World Bank Group Gender Strategy 2024–2030: Accelerate Gender Equality to End Poverty on a Livable Planet*. Washington, DC: World Bank. http://documents.worldbank .org/curated/en/099061124182033630/BOSIB17e6952570c51b49812a89c05be6a4.

CHAPTER 2

A deep dive into the EQOSOGI findings

Decriminalization

Throughout history, the criminalization of same-sex sexual activities has served as a significant means and essential component of social control through legislation (Crompton 2003). One especially noteworthy example is the Buggery Act of 1533 enacted in England during the reign of King Henry VIII. Its impact spread widely with colonial expansion, leading to the adoption of similar legal frameworks in other regions (refer to box 2.1 later in this section).

Today, about 2 billion people live in 63 countries that still criminalize same-sex sexual activities and transgender people (Mignot 2022),[1] and 1.3 billion of these people live in the countries measured by *Equality of Opportunity for Sexual and Gender Minorities 2024* (EQOSOGI). Criminalization of behavior or expression related to sexual orientation, gender identity and expression, and sex characteristics (SOGIESC) creates systemic barriers preventing lesbian, gay, bisexual, transgender, and intersex (LGBTI) people from living up to their full potential. It also prevents individuals from fully contributing to their communities and society overall, which can result in diminished economic development (Badgett 2014). Moreover, criminalization of SOGIESC-related behavior, including "cross-dressing" and consensual same-sex sexual activity, fuels the stigma and social isolation of sexual and gender minorities, making them vulnerable to violence, harassment, and abuse. Evidence from various studies suggests that decriminalization leads to lower rates of assaults and violence against sexual and gender minorities (Ciacci and Sansone 2023; Jain 2023). Decriminalization also

A reproducibility package is available for this book in the Reproducible Research Repository at https://reproducibility.worldbank.org/index.php/catalog/182.

positively affects other drivers of economic development, including access to education, improved health outcomes, and access to decent work (Badgett et al. 2014; HIV Policy Lab 2023; ILO 2015).

The Decriminalization indicator set examines the criminalization of same-sex behavior and expression related to gender identity and sex characteristics. In particular, it assesses laws and regulations in the following areas:

- Criminalization of same-sex behavior and expression related to gender identity and sex characteristics (explicitly and implicitly, such as vagrancy and public morals laws, and laws on "cross-dressing")
- The legal age for consensual same-sex relations (compared with that for consensual different-sex relations)
- Incarceration of transgender prisoners according to their gender identity.

Findings

Criminalization of Same-Sex Behavior and Expression Related to Gender Identity and Sex Characteristics

Over 35 percent of the countries analyzed in the EQOSOGI study (23 countries) still criminalize SOGIESC-related behavior and expression (map 2.1). Of the 64 countries, 22 (34 percent) criminalize same-sex sexual activities between consenting adults: 2 out of 13 in the East Asia and Pacific region, 2 out of 11 in Latin America and the Caribbean, 6 out of 8 in the Middle East and North Africa, 3 out of 6 in South Asia, and 9 out of 13 in Sub-Saharan Africa. In South Asia, for example, both Bangladesh and Sri Lanka inherited criminalizing provisions from British colonial laws on sodomy (box 2.1). This criminalization effectively bars 1.3 billion people from equal access to economic opportunity. Legal reforms decriminalizing same-sex activity, however, have begun in all regions (box 2.2).

Eight countries—Guyana, Jordan, Lebanon, Mauritius, Nigeria, Sudan, Tunisia, and Zimbabwe—criminalize gender expression and identity, and two of these countries (Jordan and Lebanon) explicitly criminalize gender expression through provisions against "cross-dressing." No country explicitly criminalizes intersex persons. Twenty-five countries have legal provisions against vagrancy, public morals, or public nuisance, which indirectly criminalize and target sexual and gender minorities (seven of those countries do not explicitly criminalize SOGIESC behavior and expression and instead rely on such indirect provisions).

In some countries, broad antipornography laws and cybercrimes laws are also used to target sexual and gender minorities. Rarely does a de jure provision explicitly target sexual and gender minorities in these laws. Instead, provisions concerned

MAP 2.1

Of the 64 countries analyzed, 23 criminalize people based on their sexual orientation and/or gender expression, and 7 rely on vagrancy, public morals, or public nuisance laws to target this community

Explicit or implicit criminalization of SOGIESC-related behavior and expression, EQOSOGI 2024 countries

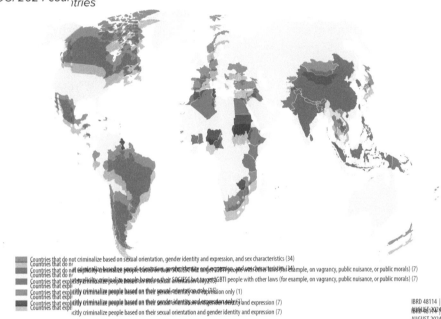

Countries that do not criminalize based on sexual orientation, gender identity and expression, and sex characteristics (34)

Countries that do not explicitly criminalize people based on their sexual orientation, gender identity and expression, and sex characteristics but target LGBTI people with other laws (for example, on vagrancy, public nuisance, or public morals) (7)

Countries that explicitly criminalize people based on their sexual orientation only (1)

Countries that explicitly criminalize people based on their sexual orientation and gender identity and expression (7)

IBRD 48114 |
AUGUST 2024

Source: World Bank, Equality of Opportunity for Sexual and Gender Minorities (EQOSOGI) data set, https://bit.ly/EQOSOGI2024_Online_Appendix.

Note: Only countries covered by the EQOSOGI data set are highlighted. LGBTI = lesbian, gay, bisexual, transgender, and intersex; SOGIESC = sexual orientation, gender identity and expression, and sex characteristics.

with seemingly neutral concepts such as public order or broad statements related to "deviancy" are applied to arrest and prosecute sexual and gender minorities in various country contexts (Human Dignity Trust 2019; IPID 2016; OHCHR 2019).

In Sri Lanka, law enforcement authorities have used the Vagrants Ordinance 1841 to intimidate, extort, and harass trans women (IPID 2016). In the Arab Republic of Egypt, the law on combatting prostitution has been interpreted by the country's high court to mean habitual sexual relations between men, whether commercial or not, and is used to target individuals of diverse sexual orientations and gender identities. The main charges include "habitual practice of debauchery," "publicizing an invitation to induce debauchery," and "incitement to debauchery" (Cairo 52 Legal Research Institute 2020; ILGA World 2020).

BOX 2.1 Criminalization of behavior related to sexual orientation, gender identity and expression, and sex characteristics: A remnant of the colonial past

---

Throughout recorded history, cultures have been characterized by a rich tapestry of sexual orientations and gender identities. Examples include the *sistergirls* and *brotherboys* among the aboriginal and Torres Strait Islander peoples in Australia, *hijra* in Bangladesh and India, "two-spirit persons" in Canadian indigenous tribes, *bonju* in Europe, *babaylan* in the Filipino indigenous community, *muxes* in Mexico, *takatāpui* in New Zealand, and *ogbanje* in Nigeria.

The colonial era was conducive to systematizing law across cultures, often to the detriment of indigenous traditions. As part of the attempt by British colonizers to set norms and standards to control the colonies, "sodomy law" was integrated into the penal codes of former colonies across Africa, Asia, the Caribbean, and the Pacific Islands. Section 377 of the Indian Penal Code (IPC) of 1860 and the Queensland Criminal Code of 1899 introduced the crime of "unnatural offenses" and became the models for the legal systems of British colonies throughout most of Africa and Asia. The Straits Settlement Law of 1871, covering territory that today encompasses Brunei, Malaysia, and Singapore, effectively duplicated the IPC. Between 1897 and 1902, administrators in Britain's African colonies, including Kenya and Uganda, adapted the IPC. The Sudanese Penal Code of 1899 also was an adaptation of the IPC. Nigeria's Criminal Code of 1916, based on the Queensland criminal code, served as a model for subsequent codes across Africa, including in Kenya, Tanzania, and Uganda.

Although France first decriminalized consensual homosexual conduct in the penal code of 1791, the code introduced the broadly worded offense of "public indecency," under which same-sex sexual activities were considered a threat to public order. This change reverberated across colonized territories. For example, Tunisia's Penal Code of 1913, enacted during French protectorate rule, introduced Article 230, which still criminalizes acts of sodomy and "homosexuality." Similarly, Lebanon's Penal Code of 1943, established during the country's rule under French mandate, introduced the offense of "unnatural acts," whereas the Ottoman Penal Code of 1858, previously in effect, had decriminalized homosexual behavior.

Sources: IESOGI 2023; Kolsky 2005; Mignot 2022; Sibalis 1996; Stephen 1883.

BOX 2.2 Recent legal advances in decriminalizing behavior related to sexual orientation, gender identity and expression, and sex characteristics—and the backlash

Advances

Although France first decriminalized consensual homosexual conduct in 1791, Peru set the stage in the twentieth century by decriminalizing same-sex relations in 1924, followed by Poland (1932), Denmark (1933), Uruguay (1934), Greece (1951), and Thailand (1957). The momentum of decriminalization picked up rapidly in the second half of the century across regions.

In Sub-Saharan Africa, Guinea-Bissau replaced the colonial penal code in 1993, and the new penal code contains no provisions on same-sex acts between consenting adults. South Africa's Constitutional Court issued a ruling in 1998 that repealed the sodomy provision criminalizing same-sex relationships. Mozambique adopted a new penal code in 2015 that decriminalized same-sex relations. Angola's amended penal code of 2021, which eliminated outdated provisions from the Portuguese penal code of 1886 and its subsequent amendments, decriminalized same-sex relations and added sexual orientation protections to some of Angola's penal code nondiscrimination clauses. In 2023, Mauritius became one of the latest countries to decriminalize same-sex behavior after the supreme court ruled that Section 250 of the Criminal Code, which criminalized same-sex relations between consenting men, was in violation of the constitution.[a]

In 2022, three Caribbean nations—Antigua and Barbuda, Barbados, and St. Kitts and Nevis—joined the ranks of nations that have decriminalized same-sex relations, followed by Dominica in 2024. The high court of justice in Antigua and Barbuda invalidated discriminatory colonial-era laws on "buggery" and "serious indecency." Barbados also struck down similar laws through its high court, ruling that restrictions on same-sex intimacy violated constitutional rights to privacy, liberty, freedom of expression, and freedom from discrimination based on sexual orientation. The Eastern Caribbean supreme court rejected St. Kitts and Nevis's 1873 ban on homosexual activity, citing privacy grounds.

In South Asia, Bhutan decriminalized same-sex conduct in 2021. In May 2023, Sri Lanka's supreme court gave the green light to a bill seeking to decriminalize homosexuality, ruling the bill consistent with the constitution.

(continued)

BOX 2.2 Recent legal advances in decriminalizing behavior related to sexual orientation, gender identity and expression, and sex characteristics—and the backlash *(continued)*

Setbacks

This wave of reform toward social inclusion has, however, been countered by some setbacks. Notably, Nigeria's Same-Sex Marriage (Prohibition) Act of 2013 imposes imprisonment of 10 years on anyone who "directly or indirectly makes public show of same sex amorous relationship." It also explicitly prohibits the registration or operation of "gay clubs, societies, and organizations."

Similarly, in February 2024, the parliament of Ghana passed the Human Sexual Rights and Family Values bill. It imposes stricter criminal penalties for same-sex sexual activities, raising the maximum prison sentence from three years to five and broadening the scope of criminalization to encompass individuals simply identifying as lesbian, gay, bisexual, transgender, queer, pansexual, allies, and any other nonconventional gender identity. In addition, it seeks to penalize persons offering support or funding or publicly advocating for the rights of those individuals with a minimum of 5 years and maximum of 10 years imprisonment. The bill is not yet enacted.

In Kenya, the family protection bill introduced in parliament in 2021 aimed to ban homosexuality, same-sex unions, and lesbian, gay, bisexual, transgender, and intersex civil society activities. If the bill were to become law, same-sex acts will carry a penalty of 10–50 years in prison.

Sources: World Bank, Equality of Opportunity for Sexual and Gender Minorities (EQOSOGI) data set, https://bit.ly/EQOSOGI2024_Online_Appendix; International Lesbian, Gay, Bisexual, Trans and Intersex Association, ILGA Database, "Area 1: Legal Frameworks: Criminalisation of Consensual Same-Sex Acts," (https://database.ilga.org/criminalisation-consensual-same-sex-sexual-acts); Yoon 2023.
a. This reform took place after the cutoff date of EQOSOGI data collection (June 1, 2023) and is not reflected in the data set.

Laws indirectly targeting sexual and gender minorities can affect participation in several areas of life—including education, employment, and access to services—and inhibit freedom of speech and association for sexual and gender minorities, groups, and organizations. The practice of these laws can leave sexual and gender minorities vulnerable to abuse and with few economic opportunities other than in the informal sector (Badgett et al. 2014).

Legal age for consensual same-sex relations

The legal age of consent for sexual relations is the same for both heterosexual and homosexual persons in 39 of the 42 analyzed countries in which homosexuality is not criminalized. China and Nepal do not criminalize same-sex relations between consenting adults, but the legal age for consensual sex is established only for women and not for men or gender minorities. In Côte d'Ivoire, the penal code establishes 15 years as the legal age for consensual sex between different-sex persons but sets the legal age for same-sex relations at 18 years (penalized as "immodest or unnatural" acts with a minor of the same sex).

Incarceration of transgender prisoners according to their gender identity

Laws and regulations on incarceration of transgender prisoners in a trans-sensitive manner are severely lacking. Transgender vulnerabilities are compounded in gender-segregated arenas such as prisons. Incarceration may, in effect, serve as a double punishment, not just depriving transgender prisoners of liberty and autonomy but also making them vulnerable to a higher risk of discrimination and violence (APT 2018; UNODC 2020). For example, transgender prisoners lack access to gender-affirming health care and face isolation, harassment, and an increased risk of life-threatening violence (Brömdal et al. 2019). These realities underscore the importance of devising laws and regulations to manage the housing of transgender prisoners in a manner that is sensitive to their needs. EQOSOGI data reveal, however, that only 8 of the 64 analyzed countries—Brazil, Canada, Chile, Costa Rica, Germany, New Zealand, Pakistan, and Spain—have enacted legal provisions that allow for incarceration based on gender identity or for placement of transgender prisoners in separate cells.

In Brazil, the National Council of Justice issued Resolution 348/2020, which established guidelines and procedures for housing the SOGIESC-minority prison population. The regulation allows incarceration of transgender prisoners based on their self-declared gender identity, to be recorded by the judge during a hearing. In 2020, Chile approved Exempt Resolution No. 5716 of the Chilean Gendarmerie, which mandates that transexual people subject to pretrial detention or sentenced to a custodial sentence be admitted or transferred to the penitentiary establishments that correspond to their gender identity, while maintaining their personal safety. Pakistan's Transgender Persons (Protection of Rights) Act of 2018 calls for management of transgender prisoners in a manner that upholds their dignity, including incarceration of transgender prisoners in separate jails and prisons. Because this mandate has not yet been fully implemented, the Sindh High Court in 2021 and Lahore High Court in 2022 ordered the competent authorities to share progress on establishment of these separate cells (*Business Recorder* 2022; *Dawn News* 2021).

Access to education

An inclusive, safe learning environment is vital for students to receive a sustained, effective education, yet schools worldwide remain a hostile space for many sexual and gender minority students. They experience higher rates of discrimination, bullying, and violence in school settings, grounded in stigma against sexual and gender diversity, actual or perceived. According to a study by the United Nations Educational, Scientific and Cultural Organization, more than half of LGBTI students experienced bullying in school settings in Europe (GEMR and IGLYO 2021). Other empirical studies have demonstrated the consistency of this pattern around the globe. For example, 68 percent of LGBTI people ages 10–35 in Japan have reported receiving insults and experiencing social exclusion and physical and sexual violence from peers in school. In South Africa, 63 percent of lesbian/bisexual women and 76 percent of gay/bisexual men have reported being exposed to homophobic jokes (UNESCO 2016). In Canada, 64 percent of students have reported hearing homophobic comments daily or weekly (Tracey, Campbell, and Taylor 2021).

SOGIESC-based discrimination, bullying, and harassment adversely affect the learning outcomes of sexual and gender minority students. In a US study, more than half of LGBTI students who reported plans to drop out of school cited harassment and a hostile school climate as the reasons (Kosciw, Clark, and Menard 2022). Sexual and gender minority students who experience discrimination and violence in school are more likely to skip classes, perform poorly, or drop out of school entirely. The discrimination, violence, and bullying experienced by sexual and gender minority students in educational settings can also have long-lasting impacts on their mental health, and they are more likely to experience anxiety and thoughts of suicide and self-harm (UNESCO 2016). Education curricula, and sexuality education specifically, often fail to include sexual and gender minorities (GEMR and IGLYO 2021). In a survey covering 108 countries and 21,000 young LGBTI respondents, 6 out of 10 respondents reported that their needs were never addressed in the curriculum or in education or school policies (Richard with Mag Jeunes LGBT 2018).

The Access to Education indicator set assesses equal access to public education of a consistent quality. It assesses laws and regulations in the following areas:

- Prohibition of SOGIESC-based discrimination against students in educational settings (including in school admissions)
- Prohibition of SOGIESC-based bullying, cyberbullying, and harassment of students
- Revision of textbooks to employ SOGIESC-inclusive language and mandatory training for teachers
- Opportunity for students to dress according to their gender identity
- Mechanisms for reporting complaints about SOGIESC-based discrimination in educational settings.

Access to education

Findings

Prohibition of SOGIESC-based discrimination against students in educational settings

Of the 64 countries analyzed by the EQOSOGI study, 20 countries (31 percent) explicitly prohibit discrimination on one or more SOGIESC grounds in educational settings. Eighteen of the 64 countries explicitly prohibit discrimination in educational settings based on sexual orientation; of those 18 countries, 11 also prohibit such discrimination in admissions. Similarly, 16 countries explicitly prohibit discrimination in educational settings based on gender identity and expression; of those 16 countries, 11 prohibit discrimination during the admissions process. Of the five countries that explicitly prohibit discrimination in educational settings on the basis of sex characteristics, three also ban discrimination during the admissions process (figure 2.1).

FIGURE 2.1

Of the 64 countries analyzed, 20 prohibit discrimination in educational settings on the basis of one or more elements of SOGIESC; of those, 14 also prohibit discrimination in the school admissions process

Prohibition of SOGIESC-based discrimination in education, EQOSOGI 2024 countries

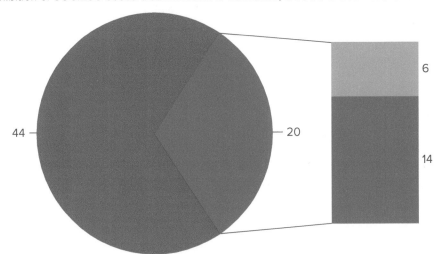

■ Countries that do not prohibit SOGIESC discrimination against students in educational settings

■ Countries that prohibit discrimination based on at least one SOGIESC ground against students or teachers in educational settings, but not in school admissions

■ Countries that prohibit discrimination based on at least one SOGIESC ground against students in educational settings, including in school admissions

Source: World Bank, Equality of Opportunity for Sexual and Gender Minorities (EQOSOGI) data set, https://bit.ly/EQOSOGI2024_Online_Appendix.

Note: SOGIESC = sexual orientation, gender identity and expression, and sex characteristics.

Among the countries that prohibit SOGIESC-based discrimination in educational settings, Ecuador and Kosovo stand out for guaranteeing constitutional protections against all forms of discrimination based on sexual orientation and gender identity. In India and Pakistan, transgender and intersex students received explicit protections against discrimination in educational settings through enactment of the Transgender Persons (Protection of Rights) Acts in 2019 and 2018, respectively. Kosovo and Serbia also extend explicit protections against discrimination in educational settings to intersex persons through recent amendments in existing legislative instruments. For example, Kosovo's 2015 Law on Gender Equality establishes the right to equal opportunities and treatment in education, among other public and private areas of social life, for "men, women and persons who have a protected characteristic of gender identity or sex determination." In Sub-Saharan Africa, Mauritius stands out for having enacted in 2008 the Equal Opportunity Act with explicit protections against sexual orientation–based discrimination in educational settings.

In some countries assessed by the EQOSOGI study, efforts to introduce legislation providing protections against SOGIESC-based discrimination have not come fully to fruition. For example, in the Philippines a bill to criminalize SOGIESC-based discrimination in educational settings, among other areas, continues to languish in the country's legislature. Similarly, lawmakers in Côte d'Ivoire introduced a bill in October 2021 to prohibit discrimination based on sexual orientation across various social and economic domains, including in educational settings. Before the bill was enacted into law, however, sexual orientation was removed from the extensive list of grounds in the bill, limiting the grounds to ethnic origin, race, color, ancestry, sex, family status, state of pregnancy, physical appearance, and economic vulnerability.

Prohibition of SOGIESC-based bullying, cyberbullying, and harassment of students

Seven of the 64 countries analyzed—Canada, Ecuador, India, Israel, New Zealand, the Philippines, and Spain—have laws that prohibit bullying, cyberbullying, and harassment based on sexual orientation in educational settings. Five of these countries also explicitly prohibit bullying and harassment based on gender identity and expression, but only India and Spain mention sex characteristics. Although Costa Rica, Fiji, and Japan have established policies prohibiting SOGIESC-based bullying, cyberbullying, and harassment in educational settings, they have no laws on these issues.

Revision of textbooks to employ SOGIESC-inclusive language and mandatory training for teachers

Only 4 of the 64 countries analyzed require revamping textbooks to ensure SOGIESC inclusivity (table 2.1). Four countries mandate training of teachers to ensure SOGIESC-inclusive pedagogy, and four countries mandate creation of

TABLE 2.1

Examples of good legal practices on inclusive curricula and sexuality education, EQOSOGI 2024 countries

Mandated by law or regulation	Countries	Example
Revision of national textbooks/national curricula in primary and secondary education to eliminate discriminatory language (such as homophobic, transphobic, or intersexphobic) or by adding gender-inclusive and nonheteronormative language (such as "students" instead of "boys and girls" and "family" or "caring adult" instead of "mom and dad") and normalizing the use of preferred pronouns.	Ecuador, Germany, the Philippines, Spain	In Spain, Law No. 4/2023, commonly referred to as the "Trans Law," on ensuring real and effective equality for transgender persons and safeguarding the rights of the LGBTI community mandates the integration of SOGIESC inclusivity into national textbooks and curricula. The law directs the government to incorporate, across various educational stages, the fundamental principles of equal treatment, nondiscrimination, and awareness of sexual, gender, and family diversity within the LGBTI community.
Creation of courses on sex education in a SOGIESC-inclusive manner in secondary and tertiary education.	Costa Rica, Germany, the Philippines, Spain	In 2017, the Ministry of Public Education in Costa Rica issued the new Programa de Estudios de Educación para la Afectividad y Sexualidad Integral, which encompasses a curriculum on sexual diversities.
Training of teachers and other school staff in primary and secondary education on preventing discrimination against students who are sexual and gender minorities or have atypical sex characteristics (intersex); or those perceived as such.	Canada, India, the Philippines, Spain	In India, the Transgender Persons (Protection of Rights) Rules, 2020, provide that the government shall provide for sensitization of institutions and establishments under their purview, including sensitization of teachers and faculty in schools and colleges to foster respect for equality and gender diversity.

Source: World Bank, Equality of Opportunity for Sexual and Gender Minorities (EQOSOGI) data set, https://bit.ly/EQOSOGI2024_Online_Appendix.
Note: LGBTI = lesbian, gay, bisexual, transgender, and intersex; SOGIESC = sexual orientation, gender identity and expression; and sex characteristics.

SOGIESC-inclusive sexuality education courses. At least nine of the assessed countries, although lacking laws or regulations on this subject, have adopted policies and strategies to integrate SOGIESC-inclusive comprehensive sexuality education into curricula. For example, Bhutan, which recently decriminalized homosexuality, has approved strategic frameworks to promote awareness and sensitization of SOGIESC through educational curricula (UNFPA 2023). All countries could address stigma, marginalization, and violence against sexual and gender minorities through holistic approaches in educational settings, including by adopting SOGIESC-inclusive curricula and pedagogy.

Opportunity for students to dress according to their gender identity

In 7 countries of the 64 countries analyzed (about 11 percent), legal or regulatory provisions addressing binary gendered uniforms, societal values, decency, and dignity limit students' opportunity to dress in accordance with their gender identity. For example, Tunisian bylaws for middle schools include detailed descriptions of compulsory school uniforms for boys and girls; and Egypt, the Kyrgyz Republic,[2] Morocco, the Philippines, Sri Lanka, and Thailand also have regulations that effectively limit gender identity expression in educational settings. In Japan, the Ministry of Education released student guidelines in 2022 that allow students to dress according to their gender identity, and gender-neutral school uniforms are reportedly becoming increasingly common in the country (Kokumai 2020; Nippon.com 2023).

Mechanisms for reporting complaints about SOGIESC-based discrimination in educational settings

Of the 64 countries analyzed, 13 countries (20 percent) have established mechanisms for reporting and investigating SOGIESC-based discrimination in educational settings. National human rights institutions (NHRIs) play a crucial role in remedying complaints about SOGIESC-based discrimination in most of these 13 countries. For example, in India, the Republic of Korea, Kosovo, and New Zealand, NHRIs are mandated to receive and investigate complaints about such discrimination in educational institutions. In Mauritius, Mexico, and Thailand, separate equality bodies are established by law to ensure that protections against SOGIESC-based discrimination are effectively upheld and implemented (box 2.3).

BOX 2.3 Addressing transgender-based discrimination: Thailand's gender equality act and the role of the WorLorPor committee

---

In Thailand, the Gender Equality Act of 2015 called for creation of the Committee on Determination of Unfair Gender Discrimination (WorLorPor committee). The WorLorPor committee has the authority to investigate complaints of gender-based discrimination—including based on gender identity and expression—and to provide victims with remedies by instructing government agencies, private organizations, or individuals to take the appropriate action. Failure to comply can be punished by imprisonment, a fine, or both. The WorLorPor committee also has a duty to compensate and rehabilitate victims of discrimination.

(continued)

Access to education

BOX 2.3 Addressing transgender-based discrimination: Thailand's gender equality act and the role of the WorLorPor committee *(continued)*

Between 2016 and 2019, the WorLorPor committee heard 27 cases of alleged discrimination against transgender people. Of those, 14 cases were related to discrimination against transgender women who were not allowed to wear uniforms according to their gender preference. In 2019, a transgender student at Chulalongkorn University and two other students filed a complaint to the WorLorPor committee after they were denied the right to dress according to their gender identities. After lodging the complaint, they were informed that, although the university was in the process of amending the uniform regulations so that it would align with the Gender Equality Act, the students would be allowed to wear the uniform for female students. The amendment to the uniform regulations at the university was announced later that year, stipulating that "students may wear the uniform according to the gender they have been assigned at birth or according to their gender identity," allowing students to dress accordingly in class, in examinations, or at formal events.

Sources: Human Rights Watch 2021; *Prachatai English* 2019; UNDP and MSDHS 2018.

Access to labor markets

Equal opportunity and nondiscrimination in employment are essential prerequisites for building human capital and strengthening economic growth. Over the last three decades, more than 85 countries in various regions have prohibited employment discrimination based on sexual orientation (Waaldijk 2021). Nonetheless, studies conducted worldwide reveal that sexual and gender minorities experience discrimination during all stages of employment: from recruitment to career growth opportunities. For example, workplace discrimination and harassment throughout the employment cycle present a challenge for sexual and gender minorities in countries as diverse as Argentina, Costa Rica, France, Hungary, India, Indonesia, Montenegro, South Africa, and Thailand (ILO 2016, 2018). According to a 2018 report, 21 percent of sexual and gender minority respondents in China, 30 percent in the Philippines, and 23 percent in Thailand reported facing SOGIESC-based harassment, bullying, or discrimination while at work (UNDP and ILO 2018). Many of the surveyed individuals believed they were denied a job because of their sexual orientation or gender identity or expression, and more than two-thirds said they had seen advertisements in which the job requirements explicitly excluded LGBTI workers (Winter et al. 2018; UNDP and ILO 2018). SOGIESC-based discrimination in the labor market reduces opportunities for decent work for sexual and gender minorities, making them economically vulnerable and pushing them into perpetual cycles of poverty.

The Access to Labor Markets indicator set identifies legislation that protects sexual and gender minorities from discrimination in employment. It assesses laws and regulations in the following areas:

- Prohibition of SOGIESC-based workplace discrimination in the public and private sectors (including in the recruitment process)
- Equal remuneration for equal work of equal value for sexual and gender minorities
- Prohibition of dismissal of employees based on their actual or perceived SOGIESC
- Equal rights to pension benefits for same-sex couples and different-sex couples
- Mechanisms for reporting complaints about SOGIESC-based workplace discrimination
- Permission for employees to dress according to their gender identity
- Availability of inclusive facilities such as gender-neutral toilets.

Findings

Prohibition of SOGIESC-based workplace discrimination in the public and private sectors

Of the 64 countries analyzed, 44 percent prohibit discrimination in employment on one or more SOGIESC grounds. Twenty-five countries explicitly prohibit discrimination based on sexual orientation in either the public or private sector. Eighteen

A deep dive into the EQOSOGI findings

countries prohibit discrimination based on gender identity and expression in either the public or private sector. Five countries prohibit discrimination based on a person's sex characteristics in the public sector or the private sector (figure 2.2)

Among the 28 countries that explicitly prohibit discrimination based on one or more SOGIESC grounds in employment, four countries—Chile, Ecuador, Fiji, and Kosovo—have constitutional provisions banning discrimination based on sexual orientation and gender identity, whereas three—India, Mexico, and South Africa—have constitutional provisions banning discrimination based on sexual orientation. Fifteen countries either have enacted antidiscrimination legislation that provides protections on one or more SOGIESC grounds in the employment sector or have incorporated these provisions into their existing labor codes and labor relations laws. Two countries—Honduras and Mongolia—have enacted provisions banning discrimination based on one or more grounds of SOGIESC in the penal code. Nepal has constitutional provisions that consider sexual and gender minorities

FIGURE 2.2

Of the 64 countries analyzed, 28 explicitly prohibit discrimination in employment on one or more SOGIESC grounds

Prohibition of SOGIESC-based discrimination in employment, EQOSOGI 2024 countries

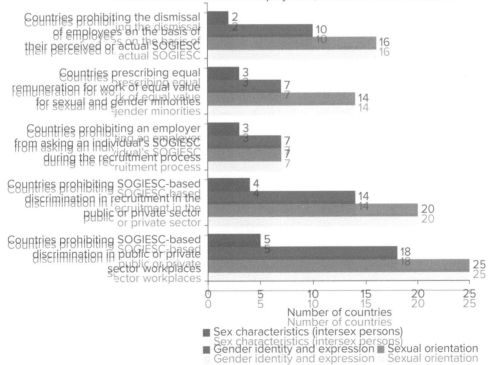

Source: World Bank; Equality of Opportunity for Sexual and Gender Minorities (EQOSOGI) data set, https://bit.ly/EQOSOGI2024_Online_Appendix.

Note: SOGIESC = sexual orientation, gender identity and expression, and sex characteristics.

as a group that can benefit from "positive discrimination" or "special measures." Although these provisions do not prohibit discrimination based on SOGIESC, they have been interpreted by the highest court in recent rulings as guaranteeing the right to equality and nondiscrimination for sexual and gender minorities. These legal provisions provide protections from SOGIESC-based discrimination across a range of employment and workplace issues. For example, 15 of the 64 countries analyzed legally mandate equal remuneration for work of equal value on one or more SOGIESC grounds (table 2.2).

Mechanisms for reporting complaints about SOGIESC-based workplace discrimination

Twenty-two of the 64 countries analyzed (34 percent) have established mechanisms for reporting and investigating complaints of workplace discrimination in the public sector based on an employee's sexual orientation, and 21 countries have established mechanisms to receive complaints about such discrimination in the private sector. At least 16 countries have established these mechanisms for discrimination against transgender persons, and 4 countries for intersex persons, in both public and private sector workplaces.

TABLE 2.2

Examples of good legal practices on SOGIESC inclusion in labor markets, EQOSOGI 2024 countries

Practice	Example
Nondiscrimination provision	In Kosovo, the 2015 Law on Protection from Discrimination and the 2015 Law on Gender Equality prohibit SOGIESC-based discrimination in public and private sector workplaces.
Recruitment	In Ecuador, the Regulation for the Eradication of Discrimination in the Labor Field 2017, prohibits any unequal treatment or exclusion of a person based on gender identity or sexual orientation in the recruitment process in the public and private sectors.
Prohibition of employer questions about SOGIESC	In Norway, section 30 of the 2017 Equality and Anti-Discrimination Act prohibits collecting information during recruitment, including during an interview, on an applicant's sexual orientation and gender identity and expression.
Equal remuneration	In South Africa, the 2013 Employment Equity Amendment Act provides for equal remuneration for work of equal value regardless of sexual orientation.
Dismissal	In Mongolia, the Revised Labor Code (2021) prohibits unfair dismissal of an employee based on sexual orientation or gender identity and expression.

Source: World Bank, Equality of Opportunity for Sexual and Gender Minorities (EQOSOGI) data set, https://bit.ly/EQOSOGI2024_Online_Appendix.

Note: SOGIESC = sexual orientation, gender identity and expression, and sex characteristics.

Of the 22 countries, most have established a stand-alone mechanism to receive and investigate complaints of SOGIESC-based discrimination. For example, in Sub-Saharan Africa, Mauritius has established the Equal Opportunity Commission under the Equal Opportunity Act to receive complaints of discrimination based on sexual orientation, and South Africa requires employers to receive and act on complaints of workplace discrimination and unfair treatment based on sexual orientation. If the complainant does not receive a satisfactory response, the matter can be referred to the Council for Conciliation Mediation and Arbitration. In the East Asia and Pacific region, Fiji, New Zealand, the Philippines, and Thailand have established stand-alone mechanisms to receive complaints of discrimination based on sexual orientation. In Korea and Mongolia, NHRIs must receive and investigate complaints of workplace discrimination based on sexual orientation. In Mongolia, the Labor Code also allows for filing such complaints in court. In Latin America and the Caribbean, Chile, Costa Rica, Honduras, and Mexico have laws and regulations in place that require mechanisms to receive complaints of discrimination based on sexual orientation. Legal instruments in Chile, Ecuador, and Honduras also extend these provisions to transgender persons.

At least two countries—Nepal and Pakistan—have established mechanisms to receive complaints of discrimination on one of more grounds of SOGIESC without prohibiting such discrimination by law or regulation. Pakistan has set up a hotline to receive complaints of gender identity–based discrimination, and the federal and provincial ombudspersons can receive and investigate complaints of harassment from women and transgender people. The rulings of ombudspersons are legally binding.

Permission for employees to dress according to their gender identity and availability of inclusive facilities such as gender-neutral toilets

Most countries have gender-neutral laws related to workplace attire, but only one requires inclusive facilities. In the Philippines, for example, the Department of Social Welfare and Development recently issued a memorandum respecting the right of sexual and gender minorities to wear a uniform of their preferred gender identity. Canada is the only country in the EQOSOGI study in which the law requires workplaces to have inclusive facilities, such as gender-neutral toilets.

Equality of Opportunity for Sexual and Gender Minorities 2024

Access to services and social protection

Discrimination and a stigmatizing environment severely restrict the ability of sexual and gender minorities to access services. Legal or regulatory protections to ensure equitable access to health care services for LGBTI people can positively affect their health outcomes and their experiences while accessing health care (HIV Policy Lab 2023). Evidence suggests that sexual and gender minorities experience disparities worldwide in access to health care, including poor communication and subpar services from health care professionals (Ayhan et al. 2019; Human Rights Watch 2018). Because transgender people are most affected by health care providers' bias and stigmatization, they avoid seeking health care services altogether, including emergency medical care (APTN 2019).

Similar disparities are also reported in access to housing and social protection, leading to further marginalization of sexual and gender minorities and compounding poverty and poor economic outcomes. The adverse impacts of lack of or poor access to social protection and decent housing were most evident during the COVID-19 crisis, leaving sexual and gender minorities everywhere isolated during those trying times. Consequently, sexual and gender minorities in most countries reported higher levels of distress, greater social marginalization, and heightened vulnerability to violence and abuse (Edge Effect 2021; World Bank 2020).

The Access to Services and Social Protection indicator set examines the ability of sexual and gender minorities to equally access services and the ability of civil society organizations (CSOs) to provide such services. In particular, it assesses laws and regulations in the following areas:

- Prohibition of SOGIESC-based discrimination in the provision of health care, access to housing, and social protection

- Access to public health insurance schemes for same-sex couples

- Inclusion of sexual and gender minorities in the national census

- Operation of SOGIESC-related CSOs

- Redress mechanisms for SOGIESC-based discrimination in accessing services

- Legal recognition of transgender people on a self-identification basis

- Birth registration of intersex children

- Blood donation by sexual and gender minorities.

Findings

Prohibition of SOGIESC-based discrimination in the provision of health care, access to housing, and social protection

Laws explicitly prohibiting SOGIESC-based discrimination in the provision of services are severely lacking in many countries. Forty-two countries do not provide any legal protections to sexual and gender minorities in access to services, and only 9 of the

64 analyzed countries—Canada, Fiji, France, Germany, Korea, Kosovo, Mauritius, Mexico, and South Africa—provide explicit legal protection against discrimination based on sexual orientation across all three domains of services assessed by the EQOSOGI study (health care, housing, and social protection). Four of the 64 countries—Canada, Fiji, France, and Kosovo—explicitly provide protection from discrimination on SOGIE grounds across all three domains. Two countries—India and Pakistan—provide protections from discrimination on the grounds of gender identity and expression and sex characteristics in the three domains (figures 2.3, 2.4, and 2.5). They also have enacted stand-alone laws to provide transgender people with protections in various services, including health care and housing. Fiji provides constitutional protections from discrimination based on sexual orientation and gender identity and expression in the provision of health care services. In 2003 Mexico enacted a federal law to prevent and eliminate discrimination, which forbids the denial or imposition of conditions on health care services because of an individual's sexual orientation or gender identity. Few countries have legal provisions that explicitly prohibit discrimination against intersex persons, but reforms are emerging in some countries (box 2.4). Although most countries provide protections from discrimination in health care, housing, and social protection through antidiscrimination legislation, Korea includes such protections under the National Human Rights Commission Act.

tries—Canada, Fiji, France, Germany, Korea, Kosovo, Mauritius, Africa—provide explicit legal protection against discrimination orientation across all three domains of services assessed by the ealth care, housing, and social protection). Four of the 64 countries—, and Kosovo—explicitly provide protection from discrimination on oss all three domains. Two countries—India and Pakistan—provide scrimination on the grounds of gender identity and expression and in the three domains (figures 2.3, 2.4, and 2.5). They also have e laws to provide transgender people with protections in various health care and housing. Fiji provides constitutional protections based on sexual orientation and gender identity and expression in lth care services. In 2003 Mexico enacted a federal law to prevent imination, which forbids the denial or imposition of conditions on es because of an individual's sexual orientation or gender iden-es have legal provisions that explicitly prohibit discrimination against have legal provisions that explicitly prohibit discrimination against but reforms are emerging in some countries (box 2.4). Although vide protections from discrimination in health care, housing, and rough antidiscrimination legislation, Korea includes such protec-tional Human Rights Commission Act.

FIGURE 2.3

Of the 64 countries analyzed, 18 have enacted legislation explicitly prohibiting discrimination in health care on one or more SOGIESC grounds

Prohibition of SOGIESC-based discrimination in health care, EQOSOGI 2024 countries

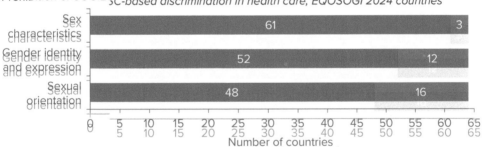

Countries that do not legally prohibit discrimination based on sexual orientation, gender identity and expression, and sex characteristics in accessing health care

Countries that legally prohibit discrimination based on sexual orientation, gender identity and expression, and sex characteristics in accessing health care

Source: World Bank, Equality of Opportunity for Sexual and Gender Minorities (EQOSOGI) data set, https://bit.ly/EQOSOGI2024_Online_Appendix.

Note: Eighteen is the aggregate number of unique countries that score "1" in any of the three questions. SOGIESC = sexual orientation, gender identity and expression, and sex characteristics.

FIGURE 2.4

Of the **64** countries analyzed, **14** have enacted legislation explicitly prohibiting discrimination in housing on one or more SOGIESC grounds

Prohibition of SOGIESC-based discrimination in housing, EQOSOGI 2024 countries

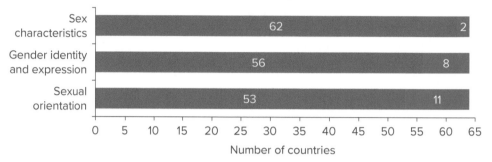

Source: World Bank, Equality of Opportunity for Sexual and Gender Minorities (EQOSOGI) data set, https://bit.ly/EQOSOGI2024_Online_Appendix.
Note: Fourteen is the aggregate number of unique countries that score "1" in any of the three questions. SOGIESC = sexual orientation, gender identity and expression, and sex characteristics.

FIGURE 2.5

Of the **64** countries analyzed, **17** have enacted legislation explicitly prohibiting discrimination in social protection and other services on one or more SOGIESC grounds

Prohibition of SOGIESC-based discrimination in social protection and other services, EQOSOGI 2024 countries

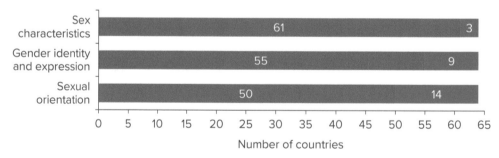

Source: World Bank, Equality of Opportunity for Sexual and Gender Minorities (EQOSOGI) data set, https://bit.ly/EQOSOGI2024_Online_Appendix.
Note: Seventeen is the aggregate number of unique countries that score "1" in any of the three questions. SOGIESC = sexual orientation, gender identity and expression, and sex characteristics.

BOX 2.4 Advances in legal recognition of the rights of intersex persons

Relatively few countries provide intersex persons with explicit legal protection, but many countries have made progress in recent years. For example, the South African Promotion of Equality and Prevention of Unfair Discrimination Act of 2000 was amended to define the term "sex" to include intersex following the enactment of the Judicial Matters Amendment Act in 2005. Kosovo, Serbia, and Spain explicitly include intersex in nondiscrimination laws. The Transgender Persons (Protection of Rights) Acts in India (2019) and Pakistan (2018) protect intersex persons from discrimination in several settings.

Nondiscrimination provisions on the basis of sex characteristics are emerging in action plans and policies related to lesbian, gay, bisexual, transgender, and intersex persons and to sexual orientation, gender identity and expression, and sex characteristics, potentially leading the way for law reforms in the years to come. The most recent Norwegian government action plan for gender and sexual diversity (2023–26) proposes including sex characteristics as a protected ground in the country's Equality and Anti-Discrimination Act. In Canada, the Ontario Human Rights Commission's 2014 Policy on Preventing Discrimination Because of Gender Identity and Gender Expression determines that the term "sex" in Ontario's Human Rights Code covers intersex. Moreover, in the absence of an explicit provision in law, provincial legal decisions have also interpreted human rights codes to include intersex.

Promotion of the rights of intersex persons should begin with an enabling framework for their birth registration, allowing parents to register the birth of a child without a specified gender or as intersex. Seven countries already do so. Recent legal reforms in 7 of the 64 countries assessed by the Equality of Opportunity for Sexual and Gender Minorities study tackle the issue of nonemergency medical interventions without personal, free, and fully informed consent. For example, in its Transgender Law of 2023, Spain banned gender reassignment surgeries on children under 12 years of age outside of medical necessities. Kenya's Children Act of 2022 protects intersex children against "organ change or removal," and Canada's 2022 Federal 2SLGBTQI+ Action Plan calls for criminalizing "purely cosmetic surgeries on intersex children" through legal reform. Argentina, France, Germany, Israel, and Uruguay also have legal or regulatory provisions protecting intersex children from nonemergency medical interventions.

Source: World Bank, Equality of Opportunity for Sexual and Gender Minorities (EQOSOGI) data set, https://bit.ly/EQOSOGI2024_Online_Appendix.

Access to public health insurance schemes for same-sex couples

Access by same-sex couples to public health insurance schemes is increasing. Thirteen of the 64 countries assessed (20 percent) provide access to public health insurance schemes that extend coverage and offer the same benefits to same-sex couples and different-sex couples. In Mexico, the Social Security Law was amended in 2023 to expressly acknowledge marriages between individuals of the same sex, granting them the same rights and responsibilities as those granted to individuals of the opposite sex. In some countries where same-sex partnerships are not legally recognized, same-sex couples have sought remedy from the higher courts to access public health insurance benefits. In Korea, for example, the Seoul high court ruled in 2023 that same-sex couples are entitled to the same spousal benefits under the national health insurance schemes as heterosexual couples, thereby granting a legal status to same-sex couples (Yoon 2023).

Inclusion of sexual and gender minorities in the national census

Only 15 percent of countries assessed by the EQOSOGI study include data on sexual and gender minorities in their national census. Immense gaps in data collection efforts on the lived experiences of sexual and gender minorities hinder progress on inclusive and sustainable development. Increased systematic efforts to collect data on sexual and gender minorities can help inform legal and policy reforms to advance inclusion, yet only 10 countries include data on sexual and gender minorities in their national census. Only 4 of the 64 assessed countries—Ecuador, Nepal, New Zealand, and Uruguay—include sexual orientation as a response option in their national census. In New Zealand, the 2023 census was the first in the country's history to collect data on gender, sexual identity, and variations of sex characteristics.[3]

Eight of the 64 countries include identifying questions for transgender people in the national census by adding various gender categories. For example, Canada's 2021 census questionnaire included an open third gender category. Bangladesh's 2022 census defines the category as "*hijra*," India as "transgender," and Pakistan as "third gender." Countries in Latin America and the Caribbean also recently expanded gender identity as a response option in their national census. Argentina allowed self-identification on gender identity in its 2022 census; Ecuador surveyed several gender identity options in 2022, including nonbinary; and, in a progressive shift since 2021 when the country was first assessed as part of the pilot EQOSOGI study, Uruguay expanded the census gender identity category in 2023.

Six countries include questions on sex characteristics in their national census. For example, on the basis of recommendations by a task force on administrative reforms for intersex persons formed by the attorney general in 2017, Kenya included intersex as an explicit gender category for the first time in its 2019 census. According to the census report, of the total population census count of 47.5 million people, 1,500 ticked the intersex box (KNBS 2019). Bangladesh, India, Nepal, and Pakistan place intersex in the third gender category, but their censuses do not ask explicitly about intersex or sex characteristics. For example, Nepal's 2021 census added an intersex-inclusive "other gender" category to those of "male" and "female." The new category drew responses from 2,928 persons, or 0.1 percent of the population (NSO 2023).[4] Although the "other gender" category includes intersex persons, the size of the intersex group cannot be discerned from the total. The low number of responses in Kenya and Nepal may be based on underreporting, persistent stigmas, and lack of sensitive data collection methods (Knight 2011; UNDP, Williams Institute, and Blue Diamond Society 2015). Consultations with CSOs on both the design and execution of censuses and surveys, potential harm to sexual and gender minorities, and management of risks relating to potential misuse of the data are elements that need to be considered when collecting data on sexual and gender minorities.

Other countries collect and systematize data on sexual and gender minorities via stand-alone or regular surveys. In Mexico, for example, the National Institute of Statistics has conducted a large-scale survey to identify the number and needs of sexual and gender minorities in the population (INEGI 2021). Canada and Norway collect data via national surveys related to public safety, health, and living conditions (Statistics Norway 2021) and regularly publish SOGIESC-related information statistics on government portals.

Operation of SOGIESC-Related CSOs

Forty percent of the countries analyzed restrict SOGIESC-related CSOs from operating freely. CSOs are often at the forefront of social change. An enabling regulatory framework is critical for CSOs to operate freely and ensure that they can fulfill their important role of fostering social inclusion, equality, and participation—the essential components of the sustainable development process. In 47 of the 64 countries assessed by the EQOSOGI study, CSOs addressing issues related to sexual orientation can register and operate. Forty-nine countries permit transgender and intersex rights organizations to operate. However, only 39 countries, or 60 percent, allow these organizations to operate freely and without any limitations (figure 2.6).

SOGIESC-related organizations are not legally allowed to register or do not operate in practice in 15 of the 64 assessed countries, with all 15 countries in three regions: East Asia and Pacific (China and Papua New Guinea), the Middle East and North Africa (Algeria, Egypt, Iraq, Jordan, Lebanon, and Morocco), and Sub-Saharan Africa (Cameroon, Côte d'Ivoire, Ethiopia, Ghana, Nigeria, Sudan, and Tanzania). In these countries, either the law bans SOGIESC-related organizations outright (de jure) or the regulatory authority has not yet approved registration of any such organization (de facto). For example, Nigeria's Same Sex Marriage (Prohibition) Act 2014 specifies that "any person or group of persons that supports the registration, operation, and sustenance of gay clubs, societies, organizations, processions or meetings in Nigeria commits an offence." In Algeria, the government retains broad discretion to refuse

FIGURE 2.6

Of the 49 countries permitting SOGIESC-related organizations, 10 impose legal limitations on their operations

Operations of SOGIESC-related civil society organizations (CSOs), EQOSOGI 2024 countries

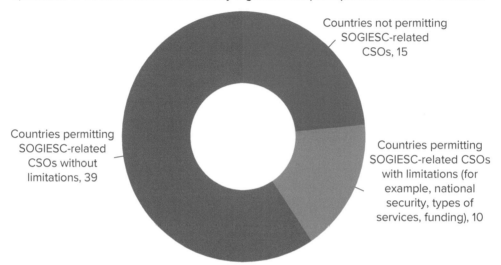

Source: World Bank, Equality of Opportunity for Sexual and Gender Minorities (EQOSOGI) data set, https://bit.ly/EQOSOGI2024_Online_Appendix.

Note: Pakistan and Bangladesh allow only CSOs related to issues of gender identity and sex characteristics, not sexual orientation. SOGIESC = sexual orientation, gender identity and expression, and sex characteristics.

to register an organization with an objective that is contrary to "good mores," and it imposes heavy fines and criminal penalties on members of informal associations. In Papua New Guinea, the law is silent on the matter, but so far no SOGIESC-related organizations have been granted formal registration and permission to run their operations because of an overarching restrictive legal environment for sexual and gender minorities.

In 10 of the 49 countries permitting SOGIESC-related organizations, laws and regulations in place can be used to limit the operation of such organizations on grounds such as public morals and national security (figure 2.6). For example, because Bangladesh and Pakistan criminalize same-sex sexual activities, organizations working on lesbian, gay, and bisexual issues are not permitted to register and operate by law; by contrast, organizations promoting the rights of transgender persons are active throughout both countries. In other countries, such as Türkiye, LGBTI organizations are allowed to register but are often required to undergo rigorous regulatory scrutiny, making it challenging for smaller organizations to use their resources effectively. Similarly, in India, the Kyrgyz Republic, the Philippines, and Tunisia, regulatory requirements on foreign funding for CSOs on the grounds of national security can also affect SOGIESC-related organizations. In six countries, CSOs are prevented from providing sexual and gender minorities with social services such as psychological and sexual and reproductive health services, preventive services for human immunodeficiency virus (HIV), information on vulnerable sexual practices, or medication and support for gender reassignment surgery.

Despite these challenges, some HIV management and prevention programs provide services to men who have sex with men. For example, in Papua New Guinea, Kapul Champions is a registered nongovernmental organization that provides HIV-related interventions and services.

Redress mechanisms for SOGIESC-based discrimination in accessing services

Sixteen countries legally mandate specific institutions, such as NHRIs, to promote the inclusion of persons with diverse sexual orientations or who are transgender or intersex. These countries are predominantly concentrated in the Europe and Central Asia region. Twelve countries have such laws and regulations for transgender people, whereas only Brazil, Kosovo, the Philippines, and Spain have provisions to foster the inclusion of intersex persons (figure 2.7). In 2023, Brazil established the position of

FIGURE 2.7

Of the 64 countries analyzed, 16 have public institutions such as national human rights institutions with an explicit mandate to advance the inclusion of sexual and gender minorities

Public institutions to advance inclusion of sexual and gender minorities, EQOSOGI 2024 countries

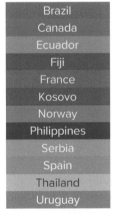

a. Sexual orientation — 15 countries: Brazil, Canada, Ecuador, Fiji, France, Korea, Rep., Kosovo, Mauritius, New Zealand, Norway, Philippines, Serbia, South Africa, Spain, Uruguay

b. Gender identity — 12 countries: Brazil, Canada, Ecuador, Fiji, France, Kosovo, Norway, Philippines, Serbia, Spain, Thailand, Uruguay

c. Sex characteristics — 4 countries: Brazil, Kosovo, Philippines, Spain

Source: World Bank, Equality of Opportunity for Sexual and Gender Minorities (EQOSOGI) data set, https://bit.ly/EQOSOGI2024_Online_Appendix.
Note: SOGIESC = sexual orientation, gender identity and expression, and sex characteristics.

47

National Secretary of Promotion and Defense of the Rights of LGBTQIA+ People within the Ministry of Human Rights and Citizenship. Its mandate includes advancing the inclusion of people with diverse SOGIESC orientations and identities. In 2021, Ecuador expanded the mandate of the Secretariat of Human Rights, a government entity, to include the eradication of all forms of violence and discrimination based on sexual orientation or gender diversity. In 18 countries, NHRIs or other specific institutions are mandated to receive and investigate complaints of discrimination in providing public services on one or more SOGIESC grounds (figure 2.8).

Legal recognition of transgender people on a self-identification basis

Legal gender recognition allows transgender and gender-diverse people to update their gender marker and name on official documents. By acknowledging a person's self-defined gender identity without imposing compulsory medical treatments or administrative processes, this legal recognition ensures equitable treatment, irrespective of gender identity. It also serves as a protective measure against exclusion

National Secretary of Promotion and Defense of the Rights of LG
within the Ministry of Human Rights and Citizenship. Its mandate incl
the inclusion of people with diverse SOGIESC orientations and ide
Ecuador expanded the mandate of the Secretariat of Human Rights,
entity, to include the eradication of all forms of violence and discrimir
sexual orientation or gender diversity. In 18 countries, NHRIs or other
tions are mandated to receive and investigate complaints of discrimir
ing public services on one or more SOGIESC grounds (figure 2.8).

Legal gender recognition allows transgender and gender-diverse pe
their gender marker and name on official documents. By acknowledg
self-defined gender identity without imposing compulsory medica
administrative processes, this legal recognition ensures equitable
spective of gender identity. It also serves as a protective measure a

---

FIGURE 2.8

Of the 64 countries analyzed, 18 have institutions that handle charges of SOGIESC-based discrimination in public services
Public institutions to combat SOGIESC-based discrimination in public services, EQOSOGI 2024 countries

a. Sexual orientation

Canada
Fiji
France
Germany
Kenya
Korea, Rep.
Kosovo
Mauritius
Mexico
New Zealand
Norway
Philippines
Serbia
South Africa
Spain

15 countries

b. Gender identity

Canada
France
India
Kenya
Kosovo
Norway
Pakistan
Philippines
Serbia
Spain
Thailand

11 countries

c. Sex characteristics

Germany
India
Kenya
Norway
Pakistan
Philippines
Spain

7 countries

Source: World Bank, Equality of Opportunity for Sexual and Gender Minorities (EQOSOGI) data set; https://bit.ly/EQOSOGI2024_Online_Appendix.
Note: SOGIESC = sexual orientation, gender identity and expression, and sex characteristics.

and discrimination (IESOGI 2018). Effective personal identification (ID) systems are a vital element of equal participation in social and economic life and in access to government benefits. The importance of this element is underscored by Sustainable Development Goal target 16.9, which emphasizes ensuring universal access to reliable identity credentials at minimal cost. The World Bank has highlighted the principle of universal access to ID, which includes the need for ID systems to be fully inclusive of and accessible to all individuals regardless of their sexual orientation or gender identity (World Bank 2021).

Of the 64 countries analyzed, 27 countries allow an individual to obtain a new ID card or passport after gender reassignment, and 14 of these countries allow legal gender recognition on a self-identification basis (figure 2.9). At least half of the sample countries in Latin America and the Caribbean allow legal gender recognition on a self-identification basis. In South Asia, Pakistan's Transgender Persons (Protection of Rights) Act is a good regional example of legal gender recognition on a self-identification basis (box 2.5). No countries in Sub-Saharan Africa allow for legal

FIGURE 2.9

Of the 27 countries that allow updating sex/gender in official documents, 14 do so on a self-identification basis

Self-identified sex/gender update allowed in official documents, EQOSOGI 2024 countries

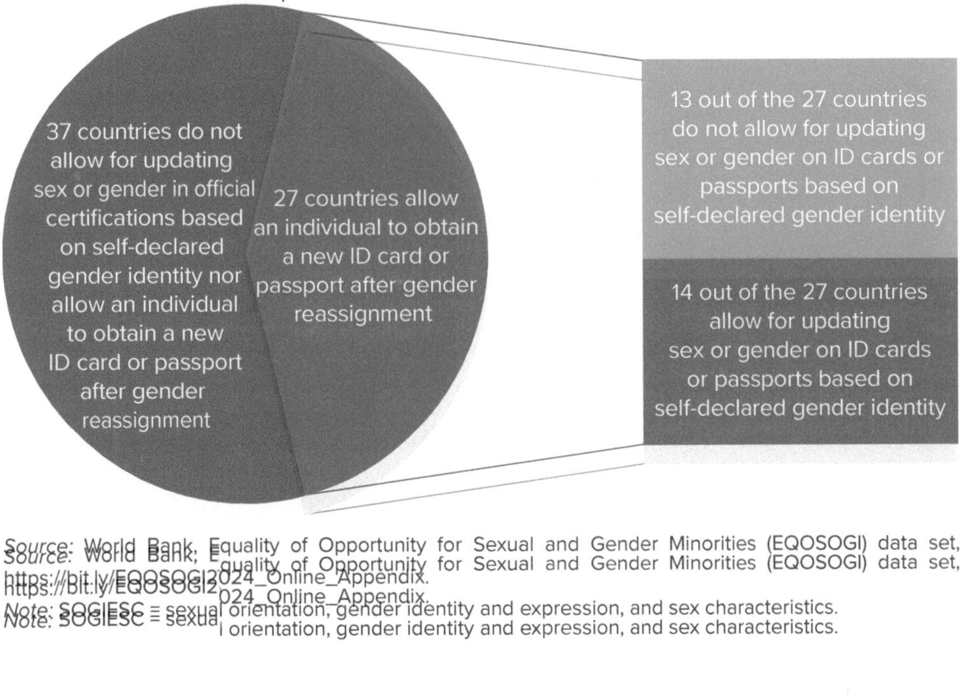

- 37 countries do not allow for updating sex or gender in official certifications based on self-declared gender identity nor allow an individual to obtain a new ID card or passport after gender reassignment
- 27 countries allow an individual to obtain a new ID card or passport after gender reassignment
- 13 out of the 27 countries do not allow for updating sex or gender on ID cards or passports based on self-declared gender identity
- 14 out of the 27 countries allow for updating sex or gender on ID cards or passports based on self-declared gender identity

Source: World Bank; Equality of Opportunity for Sexual and Gender Minorities (EQOSOGI) data set, https://bit.ly/EQOSOGI2024_Online_Appendix.

Note: SOGIESC = sexual orientation, gender identity and expression, and sex characteristics.

BOX 2.5 Advances in recognizing the rights of transgender persons in Pakistan

Pakistan's Transgender Persons (Protection of Rights) Act of 2018[a] positioned the country at the forefront of global efforts to recognize transgender people's identities. The law allows people to self-determine their gender and to have that identity recognized in official documents, including national identification cards, passports, and driver's licenses. That recognition would provide protection from discrimination in education, employment, and health care, among other sectors.

The term "transgender persons" in the act includes intersex persons and *Khwaja Sira*.[b] It also includes transgender men, transgender women, and any person whose gender identity or gender expression differs from the gender assigned at birth. Everyone is permitted to self-identify their gender without any external authorization. The act requires transgender persons to register with all government departments, including the National Database and Registration Authority. By 2022, that authority had issued new national identification cards to 5,626 individuals who had opted to change their gender in legal documents to other than male or female. The law also states that transgender people cannot be deprived of the right to vote or run for office. It lays out their rights to inheritance, in accordance with their chosen gender, and instructs the government to establish "Protection Centers and Safe Houses" along with separate prisons, jails, or places of confinement.

a. National Assembly of Pakistan, Transgender Persons (Protection of Rights) Act, https://na.gov.pk/uploads/documents/1614147088_465.pdf.
b. *Khwaja Sira* are a diverse spectrum of gender-nonconforming individuals in Pakistan, encompassing a broader array of identities beyond the term "transgender." With roots tracing back to the Mughal era, this term reflects the distinctive cultural perspective of South Asian society toward individuals who diverge from conventional gender binary and heterosexual norms. During the precolonial Mughal era, they occupied various roles, including spiritual advisers, military commanders, political counselors, courtesans, and guardians of the harem. However, this perception shifted under British colonial rule with enactment of the Indian Penal Code in 1860 and the Criminal Tribes Act in 1871, which classified *Khwaja Sira* as a criminal tribe (Shroff 2021).

gender recognition on a self-identification basis. In other countries—such as China, Japan, and Mongolia—gender reassignment surgeries are required for legal gender recognition.

ID cards in 11 countries and passports in 10 countries offer gender markers beyond the binaries of "male" and "female" (figure 2.10). For example, in South Asia, Nepal and Pakistan allow ID cards and passports with a third gender category. In Nepal,

FIGURE 2.10

Of the 64 countries analyzed, 11 offer more than two gender options in ID cards or passports

ID cards or passports allowing more than two gender options, EQOSOGI 2024 countries

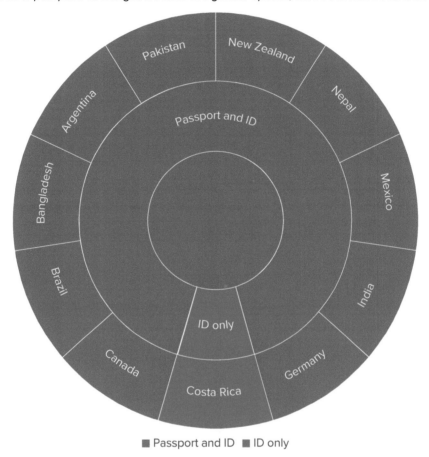

■ Passport and ID ■ ID only

Source: World Bank, Equality of Opportunity for Sexual and Gender Minorities (EQOSOGI) data set, https://bit.ly/EQOSOGI2024_Online_Appendix.
Note: SOGIESC = sexual orientation, gender identity and expression, and sex characteristics.

the category "other" was added to passports in 2015 (Al Jazeera 2021), whereas Pakistan added an "X" category to both ID cards and passports. In Latin America and the Caribbean, Argentina, Brazil, and Mexico allow an "X" gender marker on both ID cards and passports; and Costa Rica allows assignment of gender markers on passports in accordance with the gender identity of the applicant, whereas it has completely removed gender markers from ID cards since 2018.

Birth registration of intersex children

Laws enabling the birth registration of intersex children are lacking in all regions. Intersex children are severely affected when laws and regulations allow for only binary options of "male" or "female" during the birth registration process. In the absence of a gender-neutral or "intersex" option, family members and officials involved in certifying and registering a birth are forced to choose between the binary options. Challenges will continue throughout the lives of intersex persons when their gender identity differs from the sex assigned at birth in official documents. Legal requirements to assign a binary gender continue to reinforce societal perceptions and expectations that a child should fit into preexisting binary categories, reinforcing the harmful notion of a "medical need" to submit intersex children to surgeries and other medical interventions (FRA 2015; OHCHR 2023). Only 7 of 64 countries assessed—Canada, Germany, Kenya, Mauritius, Nepal, New Zealand, and Spain—allow the birth registration of intersex children without a specific gender or as intersex (refer also to box 2.4). However, some of these countries do not allow for gender markers beyond the binary options of "male" or "female" on their ID documents, meaning that children will have to choose a binary gender within the first years of their lives.

Blood donation by sexual and gender minorities

Ten countries prohibit blood donation by sexual and gender minorities, notably from persons who have engaged in same-sex sexual activity over the preceding three to five years. For example, in Kosovo the screening questionnaire currently used for blood donors asks potential donors if they "have an intimate relationship with someone of the same sex." Both men and women who have had homosexual intercourse are excluded from blood donation. Modern-day public health protocols require testing of donated blood, so these discriminatory regulations serve only to perpetuate stigma and discrimination against sexual and gender minorities.

Civil and political inclusion

Civil and political inclusion relates to a broad range of issues, including legal recognition of same-sex couples, freedom of association and expression for sexual and gender minorities, inclusion of sexual and gender minorities in countries' development plans and strategies, and inclusion of sexual and gender minorities in political and legislative spaces. Civil and political inclusion of sexual and gender minorities is critically linked to social sustainability because it ensures that all members of society have a voice in decision-making processes, feel a sense of belonging, and can actively cooperate and participate in the economy.

The Civil and Political Inclusion indicator set examines the degree of participation by sexual and gender minorities. In particular, it addresses the following areas:

: The presence of national elected representatives, cabinet members, and supreme court justices who openly self-identify as sexual or gender minorities

: SOGIESC-related national action plans

: Recognition of same-sex couples through marriage or civil partnership registration and recognition of same-sex marriages or registered civil partnerships (from other countries)

: Access of same-sex couples to adoption and assisted reproductive technology

: Prohibition of "conversion therapy" practices

: Protections for intersex children from irreversible, nonemergency surgeries

: Abolition of classification of homosexual/bisexual, transgender, or intersex as a mental or physical disorder

: Recognition of SOGIESC-based persecution as grounds for asylum.

Findings

The presence of national elected representatives, cabinet members, and supreme court justices who openly self-identify as sexual or gender minorities

Representation of sexual and gender minorities in politics and the judiciary can provide inclusive policy perspectives and have a positive role model effect. Of the 64 countries analyzed, 18 have public officials in parliament, 9 in the cabinet, and 2 on the supreme or highest court who openly identify as sexual or gender minorities, including as lesbian, gay, bisexual, or intersex people. Parliamentarians, ministers, and judges who openly identify as sexual or gender minorities not only provide representation but also can act as role models for these population groups (figure 2.11). Representation may also positively influence laws and policies that affect sexual and

FIGURE 2.11

Of the 64 countries analyzed, 19 have members of parliament, cabinets, or the highest courts who openly identify as sexual or gender minorities

Presence of sexual or gender minorities in parliament, cabinets, and the highest courts, EQOSOGI 2024 countries

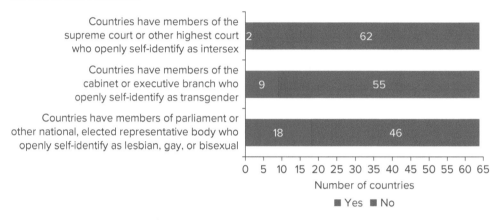

Source: World Bank, Equality of Opportunity for Sexual and Gender Minorities (EQOSOGI) data set, https://bit.ly/EQOSOGI2024_Online_Appendix.

Note: Nineteen is the aggregate number of unique countries that score "1" in any of the three questions. SOGIESC = sexual orientation, gender identity and expression, and sex characteristics.

gender minorities. For example, more widespread involvement of women in political leadership is associated with a positive role model effect and better social outcomes, including less inequality and greater prioritization of social issues, such as health, education, family policies, and gender-based violence (Asiedu et al. 2018; UNESCAP 2019; World Bank 2022). A similar effect may emerge in societies where sexual and gender minorities are represented in decision-making. In the United States, research has found that the presence of even a small number of openly gay legislators was associated with the passing of gay rights legislation (Reynolds 2013).

SOGIESC-related national action plans

Policies are an important tool for advancing the inclusion of sexual and gender minorities. Of the 64 countries analyzed, 17 countries have adopted national action plans to promote inclusion of sexual and gender minorities, either as part of broader national action plans on human rights or gender or as SOGIESC-specific national action plans. The action plans set objectives that include ensuring equal exercise of rights and opportunities; combatting stigma, discrimination, and violence; incorporating the perspective of sexual diversity into public policies and institutional practices; generating knowledge about the situations of sexual and gender minorities; and driving awareness-raising initiatives for an inclusive society.

Civil and political inclusion

Recognition of same-sex couples through marriage or civil partnership registration

Lack of legal recognition of same-sex couples limits the extent to which sexual and gender minorities can equally participate in society and enjoy economic and social benefits. In the absence of any legal recognition of same-sex partners, and especially in the absence of the option of marriage or civil partnership registration, same-sex partners cannot share equal rights and responsibilities for their children, exercise the right to inheritance, or access benefits that heterosexual couples enjoy such as health insurance and pensions, joint tax filing, and the ability to apply for immigration and residency if their partner is a national of a different country (Brown 2016).

About 22 percent of analyzed countries recognize civil partnerships or same-sex marriages. Of the 13 countries allowing civil partnership registration for same-sex couples, 14 also allow those couples to get legally married. Thirteen countries acknowledge registered partnerships or civil unions formed by same-sex couples in other countries, and 14 legally recognize same-sex marriages entered in other juris-dictions (figure 2.12).

Because of recent judicial shifts in the region, several countries in Latin America and the Caribbean have legalized same-sex civil partnerships or same-sex marriages (box 2.6). These countries have also addressed matters related to co-parenting rights

FIGURE 2.12

Few countries recognize domestic and foreign same-sex civil partnerships or marriages

Recognition of domestic and foreign same-sex civil partnerships or marriages, EQOSOGI 2024 countries

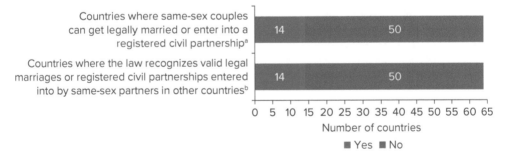

Source: World Bank, Equality of Opportunity for Sexual and Gender Minorities (EQOSOGI) data set, https://bit.ly/EQOSOGI2024_Online_Appendix.
a. Germany does not allow registered civil partnerships for either same-sex or different-sex partners. Same-sex marriage was legalized in 2017.
b. Although Armenia does not allow same-sex marriages and civil partnerships, the country recognizes valid foreign marriages and partnerships.

BOX 2.6 Advances in the legalization of same-sex marriages and registered civil partnerships in Latin America and the Caribbean

The region of Latin America and the Caribbean has experienced notable reforms in the recognition of same-sex marriages and registered civil partnerships in recent years.

In 2008, Uruguay became the first country in the region to recognize same-sex registered civil partnerships. This recognition grants same-sex couples most of the rights and benefits enjoyed by heterosexual couples, such as inheritance rights and health benefits. In 2010, Argentina became the first country in the region and the tenth globally to legalize same-sex marriages by adopting the Law on Marriage Equality. In addition, since 2015, it has allowed same-sex couples to enter "cohabitation," meaning that they can exercise the right to live together as a family without the need to get married. In Brazil, same-sex civil partnerships have been legal since 2013, when the Brazilian judiciary legalized marriage equality throughout the national territory. The supreme federal court had ruled in 2011 that de facto couples of the same sex constitute a family and must be recognized as "stable unions" under the federal constitution. In 2018, Costa Rica's constitutional court ruled in favor of marriage equality following a landmark opinion of the Inter-American Court of Human Rights in 2017 stating that all rights applicable to heterosexual couples should extend to same-sex couples. In 2021, Chile joined Argentina, Brazil, Colombia, Costa Rica, Ecuador, and Uruguay in legalizing same-sex marriages. In Mexico, the supreme court ruled in 2015 that laws restricting marriage to a man and a woman are unconstitutional; in 2022, the state of Tamaulipas became the last of Mexico's 32 states to legalize same-sex marriages. Guyana, however, still does not recognize same-sex marriages.

Sources: Inter-American Court of Human Rights 2017; World Bank Equality of Opportunity for Sexual and Gender Minorities team.

and adoption rights for same-sex couples. In the East Asia and Pacific and South Asia regions, several countries are inching closer to legalization of same-sex marriages. In June 2022, Thailand's cabinet passed a reading of four bills that propose legalizing same-sex partnerships; in March 2024, the lower house of the Thai Parliament overwhelmingly approved a bill that aims to legalize same-sex marriages (Wongcha-um 2024). In August 2022, a bill that proposed the legalization of same-sex partnerships was presented in the Philippine Senate. In Viet Nam, an amendment to the 2014 Law on Marriage and Family removed a ban on same-sex marriages. Individuals are now permitted to conduct same-sex wedding ceremonies as civil events, free from government interference or financial penalties. The state continues, however, to withhold legal protection for same-sex unions: it introduced a new provision under Article 9 of the 2014 version regarding "Conditions for Marriage," stating that "the state does not legally recognize unions between persons of the same sex." In June 2023, following its order to grant legal recognition of the foreign same-sex spouse of a Nepalese citizen, Nepal's supreme court ordered the government to establish mechanisms to register same-sex marriages without requiring new legislation. In November 2022, the Indian supreme court agreed to hear *Supriyo v. Union of India*, a case challenging the government's refusal to recognize same-sex marriages under the Special Marriage Act. The Indian Supreme Court upheld the government position that it is up to the parliament to decide whether to legalize same-sex marriages.

Among the countries that legally recognize same-sex partnerships, only eight allow both different-sex and same-sex couples equal access to assisted reproductive technology, and only six of these countries allow equal treatment regarding automatic co-parent recognition.

Prohibition of "conversion therapy" practices

Conversion therapy is an umbrella term used for a range of psychological, medical, and faith-based interventions rooted in the belief that a person's sexual orientation and gender identity can be changed. Because these practices are often undertaken clandestinely, they are underreported (IESOGI 2020; Outright International 2019). Evidence strongly points to the adverse impacts and long-lasting psychological and physical harm arising from "conversion therapy" practices, including loss of self-esteem, anxiety, depression, and suicidal ideation (APTN 2021; IESOGI 2020; Outright International 2019). "Conversion therapy" practices deny the highest attainable standards of physical and mental health to gender minorities and have deeply corrosive impacts on their overall well-being. These practices also foster a dehumanizing environment for sexual and gender minorities, perpetuating stigma, discrimination, and exclusion.

Laws prohibiting "conversion therapy" practices are lacking in many countries. Eight of the 64 countries analyzed have enacted laws to prohibit "conversion therapy" practices: Argentina, Canada, France, Germany, India, New Zealand, Spain, and Uruguay. Argentina (in 2010) and Uruguay (in 2017) have paved the way for legal protections from "conversion therapy" practices. In India, the Mental Healthcare Act of 2017 recommended punitive measures for those who use therapeutic practices against transgender and gender-diverse people. Since 2021, when India was first assessed as part of the EQOSOGI pilot, the National Medical Commission, a regulatory body for medical professions in India, has banned "conversion therapy" and has, since September 2022, categorized it as professional misconduct.

Civil and political inclusion

Protections for intersex children from irreversible, nonemergency surgeries

Few countries protect intersex children from irreversible surgeries. Only 7 of the 64 countries analyzed—Argentina, China, France, Germany, Israel, Spain, and Uruguay—have enacted laws to protect intersex children from irreversible, nonemergency surgeries. Unnecessary medical procedures on intersex children have been banned in Uruguay since 2017 by Law No. 19580. The law requires the Ministry of Public Health, all health care providers, and organizations related to health to "formalize interventions regarding intersex individuals, prohibiting unnecessary medical procedures on girls, boys, and adolescents." In Spain, all genital modifications in persons under age 12 are prohibited unless a modification is a medical necessity (refer also to box 2.4).

Abolition of classification of homosexual/bisexual, transgender, or intersex as a mental or physical disorder

Of the 64 countries analyzed, 9 still classify being a transgender person as a mental disorder. At least one country—Ghana—classifies being a lesbian, gay, or bisexual person as a mental disorder; and at least nine countries—Armenia, China, Germany, Iraq, Japan, Korea, Serbia, Thailand, and Ukraine—apply the same classification to a transgender person. Some of these countries, such as China and Thailand, have not adopted the newest edition of the World Health Organization's International Classification of Diseases, ICD-11, which redefines ICD-10's "gender identity disorder of children" as "gender incongruence among adolescents and adults" and drops it from the list of mental disorders (WHO 2023). Currently, 64 member states of the World Health Organization are at different stages of implementing the ICD-11. In Armenia, revealing one's sexual orientation during conscription could result in exemption from compulsory military service followed by a medical assessment because the revelation leads to a mental disorder diagnosis. This diagnosis then becomes a permanent part of a person's medical record, significantly affecting various aspects of the person's life such as the ability to pursue certain professions. This diagnosis also appears in a person's health records in the new digital health system.

In Ukraine, which has not yet adopted ICD-11, transgender people continue to experience discriminatory and abusive treatment from some medical professionals. In 2016, however, the country's Ministry of Health adopted a unified clinical protocol of care for gender dysphoria. The protocol was developed in consultation with local SOGIESC-related organizations and calls for removal of mandatory psychiatric assessment of transgender people before the provision of gender-affirming health care.

In Germany, efforts are under way to reform the existing Transsexual Act 1981. Once the Self-Determination Act enters into force (set for November 2024, hence after the cutoff date of EQOSOGI data collection), "transsexualism" will no longer be classified as a mental disorder, and transgender people will be able to apply for legal gender recognition based on self-identification (DW 2024; Guethlein et al. 2021).

In Iraq, instructions issued by the Ministry of Health in 2002 stipulate that a medical diagnosis of "gender identity disorder" or "transsexualism" is required before the approval of "sex correction" surgeries and that the diagnosis must be confirmed by two psychiatric committees.

Recognition of SOGIESC-based persecution as a grounds for asylum

Despite mounting evidence of SOGIESC-based persecution, recognition of such persecution as a ground for asylum is lacking worldwide. Of the 64 countries analyzed, 12 recognize persecution based on sexual orientation as a ground for asylum, whereas just 9 countries grant asylum to those who face persecution based on their gender identity and expression (table 2.3).[5]

TABLE 2.3

Recognition of SOGIESC-based persecution as grounds for asylum, EQOSOGI 2024 countries

Recognition of SOGIESC-based persecution as one of the grounds for asylum	Countries
Sexual orientation	Canada; Costa Rica; France; Georgia; Germany; Korea, Rep.; Kosovo; New Zealand; Norway; Serbia; South Africa; Spain
Gender identity and expression	Canada; Costa Rica; France; Georgia; Korea, Rep.; Kosovo; Norway; Serbia; Spain
Sex characteristics	Canada, Norway

Source: World Bank, Equality of Opportunity for Sexual and Gender Minorities (EQOSOGI) data set, https://bit.ly/EQOSOGI2024_Online_Appendix.
Note: SOGIESC = sexual orientation, gender identity and expression, and sex characteristics.

Protection from hate crimes

Worldwide, sexual and gender minorities are at great risk of experiencing violent hate crimes arising from homophobic, biphobic, transphobic, or intersexphobic stigma and intolerance. Data from all regions demonstrate that rates of hate crimes committed against sexual and gender minorities remain high. In the United States, LGBTI people are nine times more likely than non-LGBTI persons to be victims of hate crimes (Flores et al. 2022). In Europe and Central Asia, record-high numbers of hate crimes against LGBTI persons were reported in 2023 (ILGA Europe 2023). The absence of explicit protective legislation addressing SOGIESC-based hate crimes and the failure to recognize these biased motives as aggravating circumstances during sentencing foster an atmosphere of fear and uncertainty, and inhibit the active involvement of LGBTI people in social, economic, and political spheres (ECRI 2023). Insufficient legal protection against hate crimes not only perpetuates violence and discrimination but also fuels social exclusion, diminishing marginalized groups' potential contribution to the economy, ultimately exacting a significant economic toll on societies and countries, and hindering sustainable development (chapter 3). Victims of hate crimes often lose their sense of belonging to a community because they lack access to redressal interventions. Lack of legal protections from hate crimes also poses a barrier to building stronger and resilient societies (RFSL 2019).

Robust legal frameworks are essential to deter and prosecute SOGIESC-based hate crimes, ensuring that penalties for these offenses are commensurate with those for hate crimes targeting other protected characteristics. In 2021 and 2022, the United Kingdom saw a much higher percentage increase than in previous years in transphobic hate crimes—at 41 percent and 56 percent, respectively.[6] In Sub-Saharan Africa, a significant increase in violent hate crimes has been reported amid the wave of anti-LGBTI legislation across the region (Amnesty International 2022)—refer to box 2.2. In 2022, Pakistan reported the highest rate of murders of transgender women in Asia (Amnesty International 2022). At the same time, SOGIESC-based hate crimes remain underreported because victims fear being outed, and because of a lack of laws recognizing such hate crimes and establishing formal reporting and monitoring mechanisms.

The Protection from Hate Crimes indicator set identifies laws and mechanisms that criminalize SOGIESC-based hate crimes and provide protection for victims. In particular, it assesses laws and regulations in the following areas:

- Explicit criminalization of SOGIESC-based hate crimes (including SOGIESC motives as aggravated circumstances)

- Mandatory data collection by government bodies on SOGIESC-based hate crimes

: Mechanisms to monitor and report SOGIESC-based hate crimes

: Mandatory training of police, judiciary, and other relevant authorities on recognizing and identifying SOGIESC-based hate crimes

: Provision of services for victims.

Findings

Explicit criminalization of SOGIESC-based hate crimes

Of the 64 countries analyzed, 21 explicitly criminalize hate crimes motivated by the victim's sexual orientation (figure 2.13, panel a), and 17 do so for hate crimes motivated by the victim's gender identity or expression (figure 2.13, panel b). None of the 64 countries analyzed currently has legislation explicitly addressing hate crimes against intersex persons. Most of the 21 countries that criminalize such hate crimes have added provisions against SOGIESC-based hate crimes through recent penal code amendments. In at least 18 of the 64 countries assessed, crimes motivated by one or more grounds of sexual orientation and gender identity and expression are sanctioned with aggravated punishments. In some countries, such as the Philippines and South Africa, laws have been enacted to penalize hate speech with intended harm for sexual and gender minorities; but violent hate crimes, including murder, motivated by the victim's SOGIESC-related behavior or expression are not criminalized explicitly (with or without aggravated punishments).

Mandatory data collection by government bodies on SOGIESC-based hate crimes

In the absence of systematic data collection and monitoring mechanisms, SOGIESC-based hate crimes remain underreported, so the critical information on the prevalence and nature of such hate crimes needed to inform and influence legislative and policy reforms is missing. Mechanisms to monitor and report data on SOGIESC-based hate crimes are severely lacking around the world. Only eight countries—Canada, Georgia, Germany, Honduras, India, Mexico, Serbia, and Spain—have laws or mechanisms that require government agencies to regularly collect, monitor, and report data on hate crimes motivated by one or more elements of SOGIESC. In most countries analyzed in this study, CSOs, NHRIs, or police departments in large cities collect data on SOGIESC-based hate crimes.

Mandatory training of police, judiciary, and other relevant authorities on recognizing and identifying SOGIESC-based hate crimes

Even in countries where SOGIESC-based hate crimes are criminalized explicitly, legislative and policy instruments on training of police, judiciary, and other relevant authorities to recognize and identify SOGIESC-based hate crimes and provide victims with support services are mostly absent. Only five countries—Argentina, Brazil, Germany, Norway, and Spain—have enacted laws and policies that mandate training of police officers on SOGIESC-based hate crimes, and only five countries—Brazil, Mexico,

FIGURE 2.13

About 30 percent of countries explicitly criminalize hate crimes based on one or more SOGIESC grounds

Criminalization of hate crimes based on sexual orientation and gender identity and expression, EQOSOGI 2024 countries

a. Sexual orientation

b. Gender identity and expression

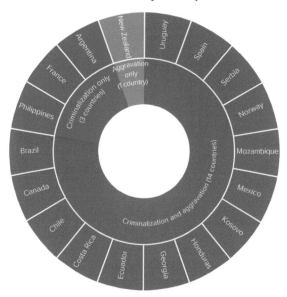

■ Criminalization and aggravation ■ Criminalization only ■ Aggravation only

Source: World Bank, Equality of Opportunity for Sexual and Gender Minorities (EQOSOGI) data set, https://bit.ly/EQOSOGI2024_Online_Appendix.
Note: SOGIESC = sexual orientation, gender identity and expression, and sex characteristics.

Serbia, Spain, and Uruguay—have enacted such laws and policies for training prose-cutors. Lack of training of law enforcement authorities can result in poor management of cases of SOGIESC-based hate crimes. Victims may then mistrust the law enforce-ment system, which may prevent them from reporting and seeking support. According to EQOSOGI data, SOGIESC-based hate crimes remain significantly underreported in all 64 countries. For example, concerns about revealing sexual and gender identity, fear of not being taken seriously, fear of intimidation by perpetrators, lack of legal protection, and harassment by police are some of the factors that deter victims from reporting hate crimes. Systemic challenges, such as the burden of legal processes and the perception that justice may not be accessible, further contribute to lack of reporting.

Provision of services for victims

Only three countries—Argentina (box 2.7), Ecuador, and France—have enacted laws requiring the provision of legal services for victims of SOGIESC-based hate crimes. The provision of forensics and medical examinations and medical certificates are mandated by law only in Argentina and France. Apart from Argentina, none of the countries analyzed in this study require offering the victims of SOGIESC-based hate crimes shelter and safe housing. Lack of support services for victims of hate crimes significantly increases their risk of mental and physical distress and vulnerability.

BOX 2.7 Argentina: Support services to the victims of hate crimes based on sexual orientation, gender identity and expression, and sex characteristics

---

The Argentine Law of Rights and Guarantees for Victims of Crimes, enacted in 2017, is a significant piece of legislation designed to recognize and protect the rights of crime victims and those affected by human rights violations. It encompasses a broad spectrum of rights, including advisory support, legal representation, protection, and access to justice. In a move toward a more empathetic and nuanced legal framework, the law also presents a tailored approach to its measures. Thus, actions taken should accord with the level of vulnerability experienced by the victims. According to arti-cle 6 of the law, the authorities must provide specialized attention to a victim facing vulnerability arising from factors such as age, gender, sexual orientation, ethnicity, or disability. This specialized care aims to mitigate the harmful consequences of the criminal act, recognizing the unique challenges faced by individuals based on their personal circumstances.

Protection from hate crimes

Notes

1. International Lesbian, Gay, Bisexual, Trans and Intersex Association, ILGA Database, "Area 1: Legal Frameworks: Criminalisation of Consensual Same-Sex Acts," https://database.ilga.org /criminalisation-consensual-same-sex-sexual-acts.

2. A provision on a unified school uniform has been taken out of the new Education Law (signed on August 11, 2023, after the cutoff date for EQOSOGI data collection) in the Kyrgyz Republic.

3. As of the writing of this report, not all data from the 2023 New Zealand census were publicly available. For available data and information on projected release dates, refer to Stats NZ, Tatauranga Aotearoa, "2023 Census release schedule," https://www.stats.govt .nz/2023-census/2023-census-release-schedule/.

4. The Nepali 2021 census included "other" gender as a response option to include sexual and gender minorities in the data collection; however, this approach poses limitations to presenting disaggregated analysis and data.

5. This report discusses only countries' national legal frameworks on asylum. It does not purport to express any view by the World Bank or its members on the scope of states' obligations under the 1951 Convention Relating to the Status of Refugees.

6. United Kingdom Home Office, "Hate Crime, England and Wales, 2021 to 2022," https:// www.gov.uk/government/statistics/hate-crime-england-and-wales-2021-to-2022/hate -crime-england-and-wales-2021-to-2022.

References

Al Jazeera. 2021. "Nepal Introduces 'Others' Gender Category in Latest Census." AL Jazeera, September 29, 2021. https://www.aljazeera.com/news/2021/9/29/nepal-introduces-third -gender-category-in-latest-census.

Amnesty International. 2022. "Pakistan 2022." In *Amnesty International Report 2022/23: The State of the World's Human Rights*. London: Amnesty International. http://www.amnesty .org/en/location/asia-and-the-pacific/south-asia/pakistan/report-pakistan/.

APT (Association for the Prevention of Torture). 2018. *Towards the Effective Protection of LGBTI Persons Deprived of Liberty: A Monitoring Guide*. Geneva: APT. https://www.apt.ch /sites/default/files/publications/apt_20181204_towards-the-effective-protection-of-lgbti -persons-deprived-of-liberty-a-monitoring-guide-final.pdf.

APTN (Asia Pacific Transgender Network). 2019. *Building, Advocating, Creating: Annual Report 2019*. Bangkok, Thailand: APTN. https://weareaptn.org/resource/asia-pacific-transgender -network-annual-report-2019/.

APTN (Asia Pacific Transgender Network). 2021. *Conversion Therapy Practices against Transgender Persons in India, Indonesia, Malaysia and Sri Lanka*. 2021. Bangkok, Thailand: APTN. https://weareaptn.org/resource/conversion-therapy-practices-against -transgender-persons-in-india-indonesia-malaysia-and-sri-lanka/.

Asiedu, E., C. Branstette, N. Gaekwad-Babulal, and N. Malokele. 2018. "The Effect of Women's Representation in Parliament and the Passing of Gender Sensitive Policies." Unpublished conference paper. https://www.aeaweb.org/conference/2018/preliminary/paper/an5yEb5h.

Ayhan, C. H. B., H. Bilgin, O. Tekin Uluman, O. Sukut, S. Yilmaz, and S. Buzlu. 2019. "A Systematic Review of the Discrimination against Sexual and Gender Minority in Health Care Settings." *International Journal of Health Services* 50 (1): 44–61. https://pubmed.ncbi.nlm.nih.gov/31684808/.

Badgett, M. V. L. 2014. *The Economic Cost of Stigma and the Exclusion of LGBT People: A Case Study of India.* Washington, DC: World Bank. http://documents.worldbank.org/curated/en/527261468035379692 /The-economic-cost-of-stigma-and-the-exclusion-of-LGBT-people-a-case-study-of-India.

Badgett, M. V. L., S. Nezhad, K. Waaldijk, and Y. van der Meulen Rodgers. 2014. "The Relationship between LGBT Inclusion and Economic Development: An Analysis of Emerging Economies." Williams Institute, UCLA School of Law, University of California, Los Angeles. https://williamsinstitute. law.ucla.edu/wp-content/uploads/lgbt-inclusion-and-development-november-2014.pdf.

Brömdal, A., K. A. Clark, J. M. W. Hughto, J. Debattista, T. M. Phillips, A. B. Mullens, J. Gow, et al. 2019. "Whole-Incarceration-Setting Approaches to Supporting and Upholding the Rights and Health of Incarcerated Transgender People." *International Journal of Transgenderism* 20 (4): 341–50. https://www.ncbi.nlm.nih.gov/pmc/articles/PMC6913601/.

Brown, J. E. 2016. "Human Rights, Gay Rights, or Both? International Human Rights Law and Same-Sex Marriage." *Florida Journal of International Law* 28 (217). https://ssrn.com /abstract=2988145.

Business Recorder. 2022. "Facilities Provided to Transgender: LHC Seeks Report from Punjab Prisons Dept by Jan 20." *Business Recorder*, December 10, 2022. https://www.brecorder .com/news/40213611.

Cairo 52 Legal Research Institute. 2020. "ElKarakhana, History of Sex Work in Modern Egypt between Legalization and Criminalization." Cairo 52 Legal Research Institute, Cairo, Egypt. https://cairo52.com/wp-content/uploads/2020/11/ElKarakhana_English.pdf.

Ciacci, R., and D. Sansone. 2023. "The Impact of Sodomy Law Repeals on Crime." *Journal of Population Economics* 36: 2519–48. https://doi.org/10.1007/s00148-023-00953-1.

Crompton, L. 2003. *Homosexuality and Civilization.* Cambridge, MA, and London: Belknap Press.

Dawn News. 2021. "SHC Seeks Report about Separate Barracks in Prisons for Transgender Inmates." *Dawn News*, March 7, 2021. https://www.dawn.com/news/1611039.

Deutsche Welle (DW). 2024. "Gender Identity Law Passes in German Parliament." April 12, 2024. https://www.dw.com/en/gender-identity-law-passes-in-german-parliament/a-68800054.

ECRI (European Commission against Racism and Intolerance). 2023. "ECRI General Policy Recommendation No. 17: On Preventing and Combating Intolerance and Discrimination against LGBTI Persons." ECRI, Strasbourg, Germany. https://hudoc.ecri.coe.int/eng #%7B%22sort%22:%5B%22ecripublicationdate%20descending%22%5D,%22ecriidentif ier%22:%5B%22REC-17-2023-30-ENG%22%5D%7D.

Edge Effect. 2021. *"We Don't Do a Lot for Them Specifically": A Scoping Report on Gaps and Opportunities for Improving Diverse SOGIESC Inclusion in Cash Transfer and Social Protection Programs, during the COVID-19 Crisis and Beyond.* Edge Effect report for the Australian Department of Foreign Affairs and Trade. https://www.edgeeffect.org /wp-content/uploads/2021/08/WDDALFTS_FullReport_Web.pdf.

Flores, A. R., R. L. Stotzer, I. H. Meyer, and L. L. Langton. 2022. "Hate Crimes against LGBT People: National Crime Victimization Survey, 2017–2019." PLoS ONE 17(12): e0279363. https://doi.org/10.1371/journal.pone.0279363.

FRA (Fundamental Rights Agency). 2015. "The Fundamental Rights Situation of Intersex People." FRA Focus, FRA, Vienna. https://fra.europa.eu/sites/default/files/fra_uploads /fra-2015-focus-04-intersex_en.pdf.

GEMR (Global Education Monitoring Report, United Nations Educational, Scientific and Cultural Organization) and IGLYO (International Lesbian, Gay, Bisexual, Transgender, Queer & Intersex Youth and Student Organisation). 2021. "Don't Look Away: No Place for Exclusion of LGBTI Students." Policy Paper 45, IGLYO, Brussels, Belgium; UNESCO, Paris. https:// unesdoc.unesco.org/ark:/48223/pf0000377361.

Guethlein, N., M. Grahlow, C. A. Lewis, S. Bork, U. Habel, and B. Derntl. 2021. "Healthcare for Trans*gender People in Germany: Gap, Challenges, and Perspectives." *Frontiers in Neuroscience* 15: 718335.

HIV Policy Lab. 2023. *Progress and the Peril: HIV and the Global De/criminalization of Same-Sex Sex.* Washington, DC: O'Neill Institute for National and Global Health Law, Georgetown University. https://hivpolicylab.org/publications/global-hiv-policy-lab-report.

Human Dignity Trust. 2019. *Injustice Exposed: The Criminalisation of Transgender People and Its Impacts.* London: Human Dignity Trust.

Human Rights Watch. 2018. "'You Don't Want Second Best': Anti-LGBT Discrimination in US Health Care." Human Rights Watch, New York. https://www.hrw.org/report/2018/07/23/you-dont-want-second-best/anti-lgbt-discrimination-us-health-care.

Human Rights Watch. 2021. "'People Can't Be Fit into Boxes': Thailand's Need for Legal Gender Recognition." Human Rights Watch, New York. https://www.hrw.org/report/2021/12/15/people-cant-be-fit-boxes/thailands-need-legal-gender-recognition.

IESOGI (United Nations Independent Expert on Protection against Violence and Discrimination Based on Sexual Orientation and Gender Identity). 2018. "Report of the Independent Expert on Protection against Violence and Discrimination Based on Sexual Orientation and Gender Identity to the UN General Assembly." A/73/152. https://documents.un.org/doc/undoc/gen/n18/220/41/pdf/n1822041.pdf?token=s8IoFbIi9LIrIgXJj7&fe=true.

IESOGI (United Nations Independent Expert on Protection against Violence and Discrimination Based on Sexual Orientation and Gender Identity). 2020. "Practices of So-Called 'Conversion Therapy': Report of the Independent Expert on Protection against Violence and Discrimination Based on Sexual Orientation and Gender Identity." Report of the Special Procedure of the Human Rights Council, A/HRC/44/53. https://digitallibrary.un.org/record/3870697?ln=en&v=pdf#files.

IESOGI (United Nations Independent Expert on Protection against Violence and Discrimination Based on Sexual Orientation and Gender Identity). 2023. "Report of the Independent Expert on Protection against Violence and Discrimination Based on Sexual Orientation and Gender Identity to the UN General Assembly." A/78/227. https://www.ohchr.org/en/calls-for-input/2023/call-inputs-report-colonialism-and-sexual-orientation-and-gender-identity.

ILGA Europe (International Lesbian, Gay, Bisexual, Trans and Intersex Association Europe). 2023. *2023 Annual Review of the Human Rights Situation of Lesbian, Gay, Bisexual, Trans and Intersex People in Europe and Central Asia.* Brussels: ILGA. https://www.ecoi.net/en/document/2087591.html.

ILGA World (International Lesbian, Gay, Bisexual, Trans and Intersex Association World). 2020. *State-Sponsored Homophobia: Global Legislation Overview Update.* Geneva: ILGA. https://ilga.org/downloads/ILGA_World_State_Sponsored_Homophobia_report_global_legislation_overview_update_December_2020.pdf.

ILO (International Labour Organization). 2015. "Discrimination at Work on the Basis of Sexual Orientation and Gender Identity: Results of the ILO's PRIDE Project." Briefing note, May 15, ILO, Geneva. https://www.ilo.org/gender/Informationresources/Publications/WCMS_368962/lang--en/index.htm.

ILO (International Labour Organization). 2016. *PRIDE at Work: A Study on Discrimination at Work on the Basis of Sexual Orientation and Gender Identity in South Africa.* Working Paper No. 4/2016, Gender, Equality and Diversity Branch, ILO, Geneva. https://www.ilo.org/sites/default/files/wcmsp5/groups/public/@dgreports/@gender/documents/publication/wcms_481581.pdf.

ILO (International Labour Organization). 2018. *Ending Violence and Harassment against Women and Men in the World of Work*. Report V (1), International Labour Conference, 107th Session, Geneva, 2018. https://www.ilo.org/sites/default/files/wcmsp5/groups/public /@ed_norm/@relconf/documents/meetingdocument/wcms_553577.pdf.

INEGI (Instituto Nacional de Estadística y Geografía, Mexico). 2021. "National Survey on Sexual and Gender Diversity (ENDISEG) 2021." Government of Mexico, Mexico City. https://www .inegi.org.mx/programas/endiseg/2021/.

Inter-American Court of Human Rights. 2017. "Advisory Opinion OC-24/17 of November 24, 2017, Requested by the Republic of Costa Rica: Gender Identity, and Equality and Non-discrimination of Same-Sex Couples." Inter-American Court of Human Rights, San José, Costa Rica. https://www.corteidh.or.cr/docs/opiniones/seriea_24_eng.pdf.

IPID (Institute for Participatory Interaction in Development). 2016. "Rapid Situation Assessment of Transgender Persons in Sri Lanka." Final draft. IPID, Sri Lanka. https://translaw.clpr.org.in /wp-content/uploads/2019/01/Sri_Lanka_Rapid_Situational_Assessment_of_TGs_2017.pdf.

Jain, D. 2023. "Impact of the Decriminalization of Homosexuality in Delhi: An Empirical Study." *Arkansas Journal of Social Change and Public Service*, January 13, 2023. https://ualr .edu/socialchange/2013/01/13/impact-of-the-decriminalization-of-homosexuality-in-delhi -an-empirical-study/#_ftn2.

KNBS (Kenya National Bureau of Statistics). 2019. *2019 Kenya Population and Housing Census Volume I: Population by County and Sub-County*. Nairobi: Government of Kenya, KNBS. https://www.knbs.or.ke/download/2019-kenya-population-and-housing-census-volume-i -population-by-county-and-sub-county/.

Knight, K. 2011. "What We Can Learn from Nepal's Inclusion of 'Third Gender' on Its 2011 Census." *New Republic*, July 18, 2011. https://newrepublic.com/article/92076/nepal-census -third-gender-lgbt-sunil-pant.

Kokumai, A. 2020. "Tokyo Ward to Let Sexual Minorities Pick Their School, Work Uniforms." *Asahi Shimbun,* January 20, 2020. https://www.asahi.com/ajw/articles/13049402.

Kolsky, E. 2005. "Codification and the Rule of Colonial Difference: Criminal Procedure in British India." *Law and History Review* 23 (3): 631–83.

Kosciw, J. G., C. M. Clark, and L. Menard. 2022. *The 2021 National School Climate Survey: The Experiences of LGBTQ+ Youth in Our Nation's Schools*. New York: GLSEN. https:// www.glsen.org/sites/default/files/2022-10/NSCS-2021-Full-Report.pdf.

Mignot, J.-F. 2022. "Decriminalizing Homosexuality: A Global Overview since the 18th Century." *Annales de démographie historique* 2022/1 (143): 115–33. https://www.cairn.info/revue -annales-de-demographie-historique-2022-1-page-115.htm.

Nippon.com. 2023. "Picking Up the Slacks: Gender-Neutral School Uniform Options Increasing in Japan." Nippon.com, April 12, 2023. https://www.nippon.com/en/japan-data/h01630//.

NSO (National Statistical Office, Nepal). 2023. *National Population and Housing Census 2021: National Report*. Kathmandu: Office of the Prime Minister and Council of Ministers. https://censusnepal.cbs.gov.np/results/files/result-folder/National%20Report_English.pdf.

OHCHR (Office of the United Nations High Commissioner for Human Rights). 2019. "The Right to Housing of LGBT Youth: An Urgent Task in the SDG Agenda Setting." Statement, Special Procedures, OHCHR, New York.

OHCHR (Office of the United Nations High Commissioner for Human Rights). 2023. "Technical Note on the Human Rights of Intersex People: Human Rights Standards and Good Practices." OHCHR, New York. https://www.ohchr.org/sites/default/files/2023-11/ohchr-technical-note -rights-intersex-people.pdf.

Outright International. 2019. *Harmful Treatment: The Global Reach of So-Called Conversion Therapy*. New York: Outright International. https://outrightinternational.org/sites/default/files/2023-09/092523_Outright_Conversion2023%20%281%29.pdf.

Prachatai English. 2019. "Victory for Trans Students at Chulalongkorn University." *Prachatai English*, November 13, 2019. https://prachataienglish.com/node/8274.

Reynolds, A. 2013. "Representation and Rights: The Impact of LGBT Legislators in Comparative Perspective." *American Political Science Review* 107 (2): 259–74.

RFSL. 2019. "FOR ALL: The Sustainable Development Goals and LGBTI People." RFSL Förbundet, Stockholm. https://www.rfsl.se/wp-content/uploads/2019/04/FINAL_FORAL_-_RFSL_2019.pdf.

Richard, G., with MAG Jeunes LGBT. 2018. *Summary Report of the Global Consultation on Inclusive Education and Access to Health of LGBTI+ Youth around the World*. Paris: MAG Jeunes LGBT, with the support of UNESCO. https://www.ungei.org/sites/default/files/Summary-report-of-the-Global-consultation-on-inclusive-education-and-access-to-health-of-LGBTI%2B-youth-around-the-world-Paris-MAG-Jeunes-LGBT-with-the-support-of-UNESCO-2018-eng.pdf.

Shroff, S. 2021. "Operationalizing the 'New' Pakistani Transgender Citizen: Legal Gendered Grammars and Trans Frames of Feeling." In *Gender, Sexuality, Decolonization: South Asia in the World Perspective*, edited by Ahonaa Roy. London: Routledge India.

Sibalis, M. D. 1996. "The Regulation of Male Homosexuality in Revolutionary and Napoleonic France, 1789–1815." In *Homosexuality in Modern France*, edited by Jeffrey Merrick and Bryant T. Ragan. New York and Oxford: Oxford University Press.

Statistics Norway. 2021. "Quality of Life in Norway 2021." https://www.ssb.no/en/sosiale-forhold-og-kriminalitet/levekar/artikler/quality-of-life-in-norway-2021.

Stephen, J. F. 1883. *A History of the Criminal Law of England*. Vol. 3. London: Macmillan. https://ia800200.us.archive.org/35/items/cu31924069583767/cu31924069583767.pdf.

Tracey, P., C. P. Campbell, and C. Taylor. 2021. *Still in Every Class in Every School: Final Report on the Second Climate Survey on Homophobia, Biphobia, and Transphobia in Canadian Schools*. Toronto, ON: Egale Canada Human Rights Trust. https://indd.adobe.com/view/publication/3836f91b-2db1-405b-80cc-b683cc863907/2o98/publication-web-resources/pdf/Climate_Survey_-_Still_Every_Class_In_Every_School.pdf.

UNDP (United Nations Development Programme) and ILO (International Labour Organization). 2018. *LGBTI People and Employment: Discrimination Based on Sexual Orientation, Gender Identity and Expression, and Sex Characteristics in China, the Philippines and Thailand*. New York: UNDP. http://www.asia-pacific.undp.org/content/rbap/en/home/library/democratic_governance/hiv_aids/lgbti-people-and-employment--discrimination-based-on-sexual-orie.html.

UNDP (United Nations Development Programme) and MSDHS (Ministry of Social Development and Human Security). 2018. *Legal Gender Recognition in Thailand: A Legal and Policy Review*. New York: UNDP. https://www.undp.org/sites/g/files/zskgke326/files/migration/th/legal-gender-recognition-in-thailand-2018.pdf.

UNDP (United Nations Development Programme), Williams Institute, and Blue Diamond Society. 2015. *Surveying Nepal's Sexual and Gender Minorities: An Inclusive Approach*. New York: UNDP. https://www.undp.org/asia-pacific/publications/surveying-nepals-sexual-and-gender-minorities-inclusive-approach.

UNESCAP (United Nations Economic and Social Commission for Asia and the Pacific). 2019. "Women's Political Participation and Leadership." Social Development Policy Briefs No. 2019/03, UNESCAP, Bangkok, Thailand.

UNESCO (United Nations Educational, Scientific and Cultural Organization). 2016. *Out in the Open: Education Sector Responses to Violence Based on Sexual Orientation and Gender Identity/Expression.* Paris: UNESCO. https://unesdoc.unesco.org/ark:/48223/pf0000244756.

UNFPA (United Nations Population Fund). 2023. "Evaluation Report: 7th Country Programme Evaluation 2019–23." UNFPA, Bhutan. https://www.unfpa.org/sites/default/files/board-documents/3.%20Bhutan_UNFPA_7th%20Country%20Programme%20Evaluation%20%282019-2023%29.pdf.

UNODC (United Nations Office on Drugs and Crime). 2020. *Mapping of Good Practices for the Management of Transgender Prisoners: Literature Review.* UNODC: Vienna, Austria. https://www.undp.org/sites/g/files/zskgke326/files/2023-03/UNDP-TH-the-mapping-of-good-practices-for-the-management-of-transgender-prisoners.pdf.

Waaldijk, K. 2021. "The Strong Global Trend of Prohibiting Employment Discrimination Based on Sexual Orientation." *Amsterdam University Press* 24 (3): 388–400.

WHO (World Health Organization). 2023. "ICD-11 2023 Release Is Here." News release, February 14, 2023. Switzerland. https://www.who.int/news/item/14-02-2023-icd-11-2023-release-is-here.

Winter, S., C. Davis-McCabe, C. Russell, D. Wilde, T. H. Chu, P. Suparak, and J. Wong. 2018. *Denied Work: An Audit of Employment Discrimination on the Basis of Gender Identity in Asia.* Bangkok: Asia Pacific Transgender Network and United Nations Development Programme. https://www.undp.org/asia-pacific/publications/denied-work-%E2%80%93-audit-employment-discrimination-basis-gender-identity-south-east-asia.

Wongcha-um, P. 2024. "Thailand Moves Closer to Legalising Same-Sex Unions as Parliament Passes Landmark Bill." Reuters, March 27, 2024. https://www.reuters.com/world/asia-pacific/thailand-moves-closer-legalising-same-sex-unions-parliament-passes-landmark-bill-2024-03-27/.

World Bank. 2020. "Stigma Is Not Quarantined: The Impact of COVID-19 on the LGBTI Community." Feature story, May 15, World Bank, Washington, DC. https://www.worldbank.org/en/news/feature/2020/05/15/estigma-cuarentena-covid-lgbti.

World Bank. 2021. "ID Systems and SOGI Inclusive Design." Note, Identification for Development (ID4D), World Bank, Washington, DC.

World Bank. 2022. *Social Cohesion and Forced Displacement: A Synthesis of New Research.* Washington, DC: World Bank. http://hdl.handle.net/10986/38431.

Yoon, L. 2023. "South Korea Court Recognizes Equal Benefits for Same-Sex Couple." Human Rights Watch, February 22, 2023. https://www.hrw.org/news/2023/02/22/south-korea-court-recognizes-equal-benefits-same-sex-couple.

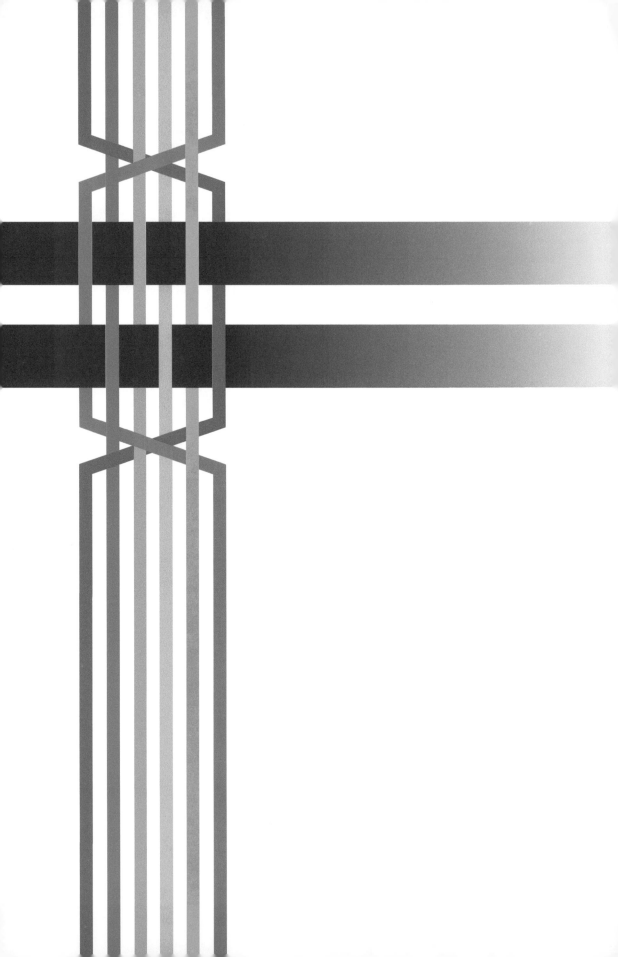

CHAPTER 3

Why do SOGIESC-inclusive laws and policies matter for economic development?

SOGIESC inclusion and development

Policies and laws that promote the inclusion of all groups in a society contribute to economic development. Research on gender equality, in particular, shows that societies in which women have the same rights and opportunities as men also experience greater economic prosperity (World Bank 2023). Several studies also reveal that gender-discriminatory laws are linked to economic outcomes such as differences in labor force participation and wage gaps between men and women (Hyland, Djankov, and Goldberg 2020; Roy 2019). For example, the removal of legal barriers can increase women's labor force participation (Amin and Islam 2015; Htun, Jensenius, and Nelson-Nuñez 2019) and help women access finance to become entrepreneurs (Islam, Muzi, and Amin 2019). At the macro level, the adoption of gender-inclusive laws can help poorer countries close the income gap with richer countries (Sever 2022). Beyond gender, there is evidence that inclusive policies aimed at other marginalized groups, including displaced persons (World Bank 2022) and racial minorities (Buckman et al. 2021), are also linked to improvements in economic development.

Gender equality is closely linked to the inclusion of persons often excluded because of their sexual orientation, gender identity and expression, and sex characteristics (SOGIESC)—refer to Cortez et al. 2023. In many countries, restrictive gender norms produce an unequal distribution of power between men and women, with men traditionally holding authority over women (World Bank 2011). Such social norms and

---

A reproducibility package is available for this book in the Reproducible Research Repository at https://reproducibility.worldbank.org/index.php/catalog/182.

unequal distribution of power not only restrict women's access to opportunities and resources but also restrict their agency and can contribute to domestic violence. Like heterosexual and cisgender women and girls, sexual and gender minorities are also affected by restrictive social norms (Heise et al. 2019). Sexual and gender minorities face punishment, violence, and other forms of exclusion because they transgress traditional gender roles and norms, because they express a gender identity that does not conform with their gender as assigned at birth, or because their gender expression is different from the norm or social expectations. The inflexibility of expectations related to gender norms and gender roles thus leads not only to inequality for women and girls but also to inequality for sexual and gender minorities (Rees-Turyn et al. 2008).

The connection between gender equality and SOGIESC inclusion is emphasized for the first time in the World Bank's 2024–30 Gender Strategy. A binary approach to gender excludes large groups of people, such as those who are intersex and nonbinary as well as those who do not abide by prescribed gender roles or gender expressions.[1] It is therefore critical to expand the definitions and understanding of gender to include all sexual and gender minorities.

Legal frameworks that promote the inclusion of sexual and gender minorities are associated with strides in economic development. Badgett, Waaldijk, and van der Meulen Rodgers (2019) examined the relationship between the legal inclusion of lesbian, gay, bisexual, transgender, and intersex (LGBTI) individuals and economic development in 132 countries between 1966 and 2011. Their analysis finds that improvements in LGBTI legal rights[2] are associated with higher gross domestic product (GDP) per capita. By contrast, exclusion based on SOGIESC has significant economic consequences. These consequences include lower productivity and output due to employment discrimination and labor supply constraints; inefficient investment in human capital stemming from lower returns to education and from discrimination and violence in educational settings; output losses due to health disparities arising from health care discrimination and exclusion from services; and the need to redirect resources to social and health services to address the impacts of exclusion (Cortez et al. 2023). Quantifying the monetary and fiscal impacts of SOGIESC-based exclusion is challenging because of a lack of nationally representative data on sexual and gender minorities. However, two recent studies on North Macedonia and Serbia estimate that the annual economic losses due to SOGIESC-based exclusion total 0.5 percent of GDP in each country and that the annual fiscal losses total approximately 0.10 percent of Serbia's 2021 GDP and 0.13 percent of North Macedonia's 2021 GDP (Flores et al. 2023a, 2023b; refer to box 3.1 for a discussion).

Although most research focuses on the link between inclusion and economic outcomes, inclusive policies also contribute to social sustainability. Together with economic and environmental sustainability, inclusion helps to reduce poverty and

BOX 3.1 World Bank research on the economic cost of SOGIESC-based exclusion

Two World Bank reports on North Macedonia and Serbia (Flores et al. 2023a, 2023b) address the economic cost of exclusion based on sexual orientation, gender identity and expression, and sex characteristics (SOGIESC). These reports are the first two in a series of studies that combine data on labor market indicators with the levels of labor market exclusion experienced by lesbian, gay, bisexual, transgender, and intersex (LGBTI) individuals to estimate the economic consequences of their exclusion. The research aims to quantify the economic and fiscal losses resulting from the exclusion of sexual and gender minorities from the labor market. These insights can further inform evidence-based policy interventions to promote inclusivity and reduce discrimination.

Methodology

To estimate the economic cost of exclusion, the reports present two theoretical models addressing labor market and related issues. The first model estimates the accumulated wage losses experienced by LGBTI individuals because of their exclusion from the labor market. It factors in the lower wages stemming from the inability of employed LGBTI individuals to fully use their human capital, the higher unemployment leading to associated wage losses, and the reduced labor force participation or greater inactivity resulting in wage losses. This model focuses on quantifying the direct economic losses incurred by LGBTI individuals in terms of reduced incomes and labor productivity due to exclusion from employment opportunities.

The second model estimates the fiscal losses arising from the lower income and payroll taxes stemming from the reduced employment opportunities for LGBTI individuals, as well as the higher expenditures on unemployment benefits and active labor market programs. This model adapts a World Bank framework originally used to estimate the costs of the exclusion of Roma from the labor market. Unlike the wage losses model, the fiscal impact model focuses on quantifying the broader fiscal implications of SOGIESC-based exclusion, including its effects on government revenue and expenditures related to social welfare programs and labor market interventions.

Key Findings

: LGBTI individuals—especially those individuals subject to higher levels of workplace discrimination and stigma—experience higher unemployment rates than the general population. In Serbia in 2021, the unemployment rate among LGBTI individuals was 17.5 percent, significantly higher than the general population's

(continued)

BOX 3.1 World Bank research on the economic cost of
SOGIESC-based exclusion *(continued)*

rate of 7.2 percent. In North Macedonia in the same year, the unemployment rate among LGBTI individuals was 13.5 percent, compared with the general population's rate of 12.0 percent.

- Workplace discrimination patterns vary among segments of the LGBTI community. In North Macedonia, bisexual and intersex individuals report experiencing more discrimination; in Serbia, transgender and intersex individuals report higher levels of discrimination.

- LGBTI individuals reporting the highest levels of workplace discrimination and stigma also experience the most pronounced wage losses.

- The annual economic and fiscal losses arising from SOGIESC-based exclusion are estimated to be substantial, totaling 0.5 percent of gross domestic product for economic losses in each country, and approximately 0.1 percent of gross domestic product for fiscal losses in Serbia and 0.13 percent of gross domestic product in North Macedonia (for additional details on the total economic cost, refer to figure B3.1.1).

FIGURE B3.1.1

Total economic and fiscal cost of LGBTI exclusion in North Macedonia and Serbia, 2021

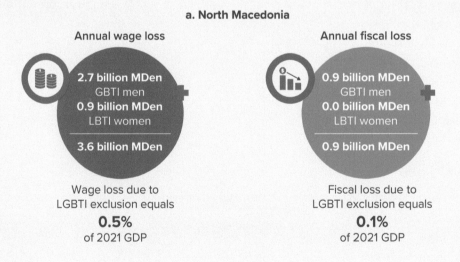

a. North Macedonia

Annual wage loss

2.7 billion MDen
GBTI men
0.9 billion MDen
LBTI women

3.6 billion MDen

Wage loss due to
LGBTI exclusion equals
0.5%
of 2021 GDP

Annual fiscal loss

0.9 billion MDen
GBTI men
0.0 billion MDen
LBTI women

0.9 billion MDen

Fiscal loss due to
LGBTI exclusion equals
0.1%
of 2021 GDP

(continued)

BOX 3.1 World Bank research on the economic cost of
SOGIESC-based exclusion *(continued)*

FIGURE B3.1.1

**Total economic and fiscal cost of LGBTI exclusion in North Macedonia and
Serbia, 2021 (*continued*)**

b. Serbia

Annual wage loss

12.4 billion SRD
GBTI men
18.7 billion SRD
LBTI women

31.1 billion SRD

Wage loss due to
LGBTI exclusion equals
0.5%
of 2021 GDP

Annual fiscal loss

4.5 billion SRD
GBTI men
4.9 billion SRD
LBTI women

9.4 billion SRD

Fiscal loss due to
LGBTI exclusion equals
0.1%
of 2021 GDP

Sources: Flores 2023a, 2023b.
Note: GBTI = gay, bisexual, transgender, and intersex; GDP = gross domestic product; LBTI = lesbian,
bisexual, transgender, and intersex; LGBTI = lesbian, gay, bisexual, transgender, and intersex; Mden = North
Macedonian denar; SRD = Serbian dinar.

promote growth by enabling communities to work together to overcome challenges, deliver public goods, and allocate scarce resources in ways perceived to
be legitimate and fair so that all people can thrive over time (Barron et al. 2023).
Inclusion is one of four key components of social sustainability. The other components are social cohesion, resilience, and process legitimacy. Although each of
these components has innate value in much the same way as peace, freedom,
or sovereignty, each also has instrumental value for supporting poverty reduction and inclusive growth. Cross-country analysis finds that these components are
positively correlated with poverty reduction, human capital, human development,
and equality, and that inclusion has an especially strong correlation with poverty
reduction and human capital (Barron et al. 2023). Therefore, laws and policies
promoting LGBTI inclusion will likely also contribute to improved social sustainability by increasing the degree to which more people feel part of the development process and believe they will benefit from it.

Three pathways connecting SOGIESC inclusion and development outcomes

This report focuses on three pathways through which SOGIESC inclusion is connected to economic development and social sustainability: human capital, investments and innovation, and lived experience. Figure 3.1 summarizes the connection between SOGIESC inclusion, as measured by the Equality of Opportunity for Sexual and Gender Minorities (EQOSOGI) score; the three pathways; and economic development and social sustainability outcomes.[3] Although the framework highlights the connection between SOGIESC inclusion and development outcomes, it is plausible and likely that improved development also contributes to SOGIESC inclusion. The framework and analysis in this chapter illustrate the likely connection between SOGIESC inclusion and development outcomes, but the chapter does not propose a causal link between the two.

Pathway 1: SOGIESC inclusion may improve human capital by generating opportunities for sexual and gender minorities to access quality education, health care, and jobs in nondiscriminatory settings. Human capital consists of the knowledge, skills, and health that people accumulate over their lifetime (World Bank 2021). In addition to their intrinsic value, knowledge, skills, and health also enable people to participate productively in the economy. Inclusive policies are therefore critical to ensuring that all individuals can both access the means of accumulating human capital and use their accumulated capital.[4]

Sexual and gender minorities face barriers in education and health settings that can limit their human capital accumulation and contributions to the economy.

FIGURE 3.1

Pathways linking SOGIESC inclusion with economic development and social sustainability

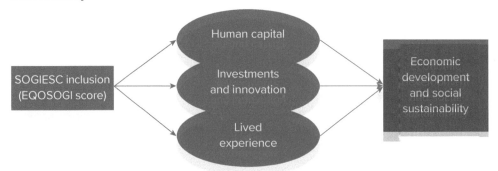

Source: World Bank Equality of Opportunity for Sexual and Gender Minorities (EQOSOGI) team.
Note: SOGIESC = sexual orientation, gender identity and expression, and sex characteristics.

LGBTI students frequently face discrimination in educational settings, including unequal treatment, bullying and harassment, and exclusion from certain activities (Khan, Bondyopadhyay, and Mulji 2005; Kosciw, Clark, and Menard 2022; UNESCO 2012, 2015). Such discrimination can drive sexual and gender minority students to drop out of school, skip classes and activities, and refrain from pursuing higher levels of education (Badgett, Waaldijk, and van der Meulen Rodgers 2019; Human Rights Watch 2016). In health care, LGBTI individuals often face higher health risks while also receiving inadequate care and access because of stigma, lack of awareness of LGBTI health issues among health care providers, and inadequate training or policies on LGBTI health (Hafeez et al. 2017). Transgender and intersex individuals, in particular, often report difficulties accessing the appropriate and required health care (Haghighat et al. 2023; UNDP 2023). Overall, policies and social norms that prevent or deter LGBTI persons from obtaining equal, high-quality education and health care can reduce their productivity and labor force participation, and ultimately impede economic output and growth (Badgett 2014).

Discrimination and violence in the workplace and in other settings can also lead to lower productivity, poor physical and mental health, and higher health care and social protection costs. LGBTI persons often experience discrimination in the hiring process (FRA 2020; O'Malley and Holzinger 2018; World Bank 2018); in many places, the unemployment rate among LGBTI individuals is much higher than that of the general population (Flores et al. 2023a, 2023b). Within the workplace, discrimination and harassment adversely affect the mental and physical health, wages, and productivity of sexual and gender minorities (Sears and Mallory 2011). LGBTI people are then placed in less qualified roles, particularly in the informal sector (Badgett, Waaldijk, and van der Meulen Rodgers 2019). Overall, discrimination and harassment limit the ability of LGBTI persons to apply their full human capital and to access new human capital that comes from on-the-job learning. Violence and discrimination can also lead to lower life expectancy, which not only affects the productivity of LGBTI persons but also leads to higher health care and social protection costs and lower incentives to invest in human capital (Becker 1971; Bergmann 1971; OECD 2020). Variables in the EQOSOGI indicator sets on Access to Education, Access to Labor Markets, and Access to Services and Social Protection are especially linked to the human capital pathway to development outcomes.

Pathway 2: SOGIESC inclusion may stimulate increased private investments and innovation by, for example, signaling to investors an openness to business. Although it is unlikely that LGBTI inclusion alone explains most investments, inclusive policies can enhance a "country's attractiveness to tourists, potential foreign investors, or other trading partners" (Badgett, Waaldijk, and van der Meulen Rodgers 2019). For example, Noland (2005) finds a positive relationship between positive attitudes toward homosexuals and foreign direct investment flows in

44 countries from 1997 to 2002. Vadlamannati, Janz, and Berntsen (2018) suggest that foreign investors may avoid countries that the United Nations Human Rights Council has criticized for human rights violations. In addition to investments, SOGIESC inclusion may drive innovation and economic output. Florida and Gates (2001) examined the connection between a metropolitan area's tolerance and diversity and its ability to attract high-technology industries. Their study finds a strong correlation between a large gay population, among other factors, and the success of high-technology industries in an area. The research underscores the role of tolerance and diversity in attracting talent and promoting economic growth in the technology sector. Other studies also highlight the positive correlation between employer policies supporting LGBTI workers and financial indicators (Fatmy et al. 2022; Li and Nagar 2013; Shan, Fu, and Zheng 2017). In a study focusing on US companies from 2003 to 2016, Fatmy et al. (2022) reveal that those companies with more progressive LGBTI policies tend to have higher profitability and stock market valuations. Shan, Fu, and Zheng (2017) investigated corporate sexual equality, finding a positive relationship between such policies and higher stock returns and market valuations in US public firms from 2002 to 2006. Meanwhile, a report by Open For Business finds that a society's SOGIESC inclusiveness contributes to improved economic, business, and individual performance (Miller and Parker 2015). Variables from the EQOSOGI indicator sets on Access to Labor Markets, Civil and Political Inclusion, and Protection from Hate Crimes are especially connected to the investments and innovation pathway to development outcomes.

Pathway 3: SOGIESC inclusion can improve the lived experience of sexual and gender minorities, and this experience, or freedom, promotes development. This pathway builds on the argument by Sen (1999) that development is not just about wealth but also about individuals having the freedom to choose how they lead their lives. When laws, policies, and social norms discriminate against or exclude sexual and gender minorities, those minorities have limited freedom to make choices about how they live their lives—in other words, their lived experience is negatively affected. This pathway differs from the human capital approach because it goes beyond having access to the education or jobs needed to increase and use capital and instead focuses more on living in an environment where people feel free to choose how to "convert equal access to goods and services into the actual achievement of what they want to do and be" (Badgett, Waaldijk, and van der Meulen Rodgers 2019, 4). Discrimination, violence, exclusionary policies, and harmful social norms persist across low-, middle-, and high-income countries, constraining the ability of sexual and gender minorities to make such choices. The lived experience pathway has an especially strong connection to social sustainability because a society's inclusiveness contributes not only to individual- and national-level welfare outcomes (such as wages and GDP) but also to improved agency and dignity (Barron et al. 2023; Das, Fisiy, and Kyte 2013). Variables in all the EQOSOGI indicator sets are connected to the lived experience pathway to development outcomes.

Empirical findings on EQOSOGI and development outcomes

Wealthier countries tend to be more inclusive of sexual and gender minorities across all six indicator sets. A statistically significant positive correlation (0.55) between per capita real GDP and the overall EQOSOGI score suggests that richer countries are more inclusive of sexual and gender minorities and that, conversely, countries with greater inclusion tend to be wealthier. This pattern is present across all indicator sets, with statistically significant positive correlations of per capita real GDP ranging from 0.37 for Decriminalization and Protection from Hate Crimes to 0.63 for Civil and Political Inclusion (table 3.1). By SOGIESC group, there is also a positive and significant association that is slightly weaker for the intersex group (0.42) than for the lesbian, gay, and bisexual (LGB) group (0.60). These findings are in line with those reported by Badgett, Waaldijk, and van der Meulen Rodgers (2019) indicating a positive correlation between LGBTI inclusion and economic development as measured by per capita real GDP.

Higher levels of human capital are correlated with more inclusive environments for sexual and gender minorities. A statistically significant positive correlation (0.60) is observed between the Human Capital Index and the overall EQOSOGI score, suggesting that environments supportive of sexual and gender minorities are also conducive to human capital growth (table 3.1). This pattern is consistent across all indicator sets for the LGB and transgender groups, with Access to Labor Markets showing the lowest association for the transgender group (0.34) and the highest association for the LGB group (0.61). Statistically significant and positive correlations are identified for the intersex group but are confined to specific indicator sets: Decriminalization, Access to Services and Social Protection, and Civil and Political Inclusion. These results highlight the intrinsic connection between enhancing human capital and inclusive regulatory frameworks. According to Vu (2021), the creation of a pro-inclusion regulatory framework is a well-known driver of human capital development. Such an environment signals a society's acceptance of diversity, innovation, and tolerance, which, in turn, attracts higher inflows of human capital.

Greater levels of citizens' voice and accountability foster the inclusion of sexual and gender minorities. A statistically significant positive correlation (0.67) between Worldwide Governance Indicators estimates (Voice and Accountability) and the overall EQOSOGI score underscores the importance of citizens' voices and the promotion of greater inclusion (table 3.1). Greater participation by citizens in selecting their government—as well as freedom of expression, freedom of association, and a free media—is associated with the inclusion of sexual and gender minorities. This association is present across all six indicator sets and all SOGIESC groups, except the intersex group in Access to Education, Access to Labor Markets, and Protection from Hate Crimes. The highest correlation is found for Civil and Political Inclusion for the

TABLE 3.1

Correlation analysis between EQOSOGI scores and selected covariates

Covariate	Total	Decriminalization	Access to Education	Access to Labor Markets	Access to Services and Social Protection	Civil and Political Inclusion	Protection from Hate Crimes
Overall							
Per capita real GDP (constant 2015 US$)	0.535***	0.737***	0.339***	0.048***	0.252***	0.363***	0.737***
Gini index	0.09	0.11	0.000	-0.07	0.02	0.19	0.23
Human Capital index	0.630***	0.252***	0.242***	0.048***	0.757***	0.559***	0.939***
Voice and Accountability estimate	0.767***	0.747***	0.545***	0.535***	0.565***	0.873***	0.747***
Lesbian, gay, and bisexual							
Per capita real GDP (constant 2015 US$)	0.630***	0.131***	0.747***	0.232***	0.536***	0.464***	0.242***
Gini index	0.15	0.07	0.07	0.10	0.14	0.20	0.23
Human Capital index	0.636***	0.530***	0.530***	0.616***	0.630***	0.630***	0.242***
Voice and Accountability estimate	0.717***	0.410***	0.533***	0.668***	0.707***	0.873***	0.530***
Transgender							
Per capita real GDP (constant 2015 US$)	0.530***	0.737***	0.535***	0.232***	0.545***	0.539***	0.535***
Gini index	0.101	0.09	-0.03	-0.19	-0.04	0.16	0.20
Human Capital index	0.535***	0.444***	0.434***	0.434***	0.515***	0.636***	0.838***
Voice and Accountability estimate	0.939***	0.949***	0.410***	0.434***	0.535***	0.717***	0.343***
Intersex							
Per capita real GDP (constant 2015 US$)	0.402***	0.400***	0.06	-0.001	0.337***	0.663***	0.11
Gini index	0.05	0.09	-0.08	-0.17	0.00	0.18	0.20
Human Capital index	0.444***	0.339***	0.44	0.00	0.443***	0.588***	0.66
Voice and Accountability estimate	0.553***	0.445***	0.18	0.08	0.550***	0.666***	0.88

Source: World Bank Equality of Opportunity for Sexual and Gender Minorities (EQOSOGI) team, using EQOSOGI data set.

Note: SSOGI = sexual orientation, gender identity, and expression, and sex characteristics.

* $p < .10$; ** $p < .05$; *** $p < .01$.

LGB group (0.73) and the lowest for Access to Labor Markets for the transgender group (0.34). These results suggest that democratic governance, which involves mechanisms to protect and uphold the rights of all citizens, including marginalized groups, is linked to greater inclusivity and equality for sexual and gender minorities.

Income inequality and EQOSOGI scores do not show the expected negative linear relationship: The correlation between EQOSOGI scores and income distribution as measured by the Gini index turns out to be not statistically significant (table 3.1), indicating a more complex, possibly nonlinear dynamic between sexual and gender minority inclusion and income distribution. The absence of a linear association is also present by indicator set and SOGIESC group.

These empirical findings on EQOSOGI and its association with development outcomes highlight the importance of a holistic policy framework that accounts for their interconnection. In designing policies aiming for greater equality of opportunities for sexual and gender minorities, such a framework should encompass not only economic growth but also less income inequality and greater voice and accountability in societies. That said, the analysis presented here is purely associative and does not claim causality. Future EQOSOGI reports will build on this analysis and use panel data to study possible causality. Refer to box 3.1 for two examples of World Bank reports estimating the economic consequences of SOGIESC exclusion.

These reports emphasize the importance of collecting data on key labor market indicators and on the self-reported experiences of discrimination and stigma against sexual and gender minorities. Such data collection can provide valuable insights into the challenges faced by this community and support evidence-based policy interventions aimed at fostering inclusivity and addressing discrimination. The research suggests that reducing stigma and discriminatory incidents among sexual and gender minorities could have a substantial positive impact on the economy. Recommendations include enforcing existing legal safeguards against discrimination, enhancing legal protections for sexual and gender minorities across various sectors, and reducing societal SOGIESC-based stigma.

Notes

1. The Office of the United Nations High Commissioner for Human Rights, "The struggle of trans and gender-diverse persons," https://www.ohchr.org/en/special-procedures/ie-sexual-orientation-and-gender-identity/struggle-trans-and-gender-diverse-persons.
2. The analysis in Badgett, Waaldijk, and van der Meulen Rodgers (2019) relies on data from the Global Index on Legal Recognition of Homosexual Orientation and includes eight categories related to the decriminalization of homosexual acts, antidiscrimination legislation, and partnership rights: (1) Legality of consensual homosexual acts between adults; (2) Equal age limits for consensual homosexual and heterosexual acts; (3) Explicit

legal prohibition of sexual orientation discrimination in employment; (4) Explicit legal pro-hibition of sexual orientation discrimination regarding goods and/or services; (5) Legal recognition of the nonregistered cohabitation of same-sex couples; (6) Availability of registered partnership for same-sex couples; (7) Possibility of second-parent and/or joint adoption by same-sex partners; and (8) Legal option of marriage for same-sex couples.

3. This section builds on a similar framework outlined in Badgett, Waaldijk, and van der Meulen Rodgers (2019).

4. For example, policies such as providing childcare and parental leave can enable women to enter the workforce and use their human capital (Olivetti and Petrongolo 2017). For more on the importance of human capital use, refer to Pennings (2020) and World Bank (2021).

References

Amin, M., and A. Islam. 2015. "Does Mandating Nondiscrimination in Hiring Practices Influence Women's Employment? Evidence Using Firm-Level Data." *Feminist Economics* 21 (4): 28–60.

Badgett, M. V. L. 2014. *The Economic Cost of Stigma and the Exclusion of LGBT People: A Case Study of India.* Washington, DC: World Bank. http://documents.worldbank.org/curated/en/527261468035379692 /The-economic-cost-of-stigma-and-the-exclusion-of-LGBT-people-a-case-study-of-India.

Badgett, M. V. L., K. Waaldijk, and Y. van der Meulen Rodgers. 2019. "The Relationship between LGBT Inclusion and Economic Development: Macro-Level Evidence." *World Development* 120: 1–14.

Barron, P., L. Cord, J. Cuesta, S. A. Espinoza, G. Larson, and M. Woolcock. 2023. *Social Sustainability in Development: Meeting the Challenges of the 21st Century.* New Frontiers of Social Policy. Washington, DC: World Bank.

Becker, G. 1971. *The Economics of Discrimination.* 2nd ed. Chicago: University of Chicago Press.

Bergmann, B. 1971. "The Effect on White Incomes of Discrimination in Employment." *Journal of Political Economy* 79 (2): 294–313.

Buckman, S. R., L. Y. Choi, M. C. Daly, and L. M. Seitelman. 2021. "The Economic Gains from Equity." *Brookings Papers on Economic Activity* 2021 (2): 71–139.

Cortez, C., T. Rana, R. Z. Nasir, and J. Arzinos. 2023. "Sexual Orientation and Gender Identity (SOGI) Inclusion and Gender Equality." Gender Thematic Policy Notes Series: Evidence and Practice Note, World Bank, Washington, DC.

Das, M. B., C. F. Fisiy, and R. Kyte. 2013. *Inclusion Matters: The Foundation for Shared Prosperity.* New Frontiers of Social Policy. Washington, DC: World Bank. https://documents1.worldbank .org/curated/en/114561468154469371/pdf/Inclusion-matters-the-foundation-for-shared -prosperity.pdf.

Fatmy, V., J. Kihn, J. Sihvonen, and S. Vähämaa. 2022. "Does Lesbian and Gay Friendliness Pay Off? A New Look at LGBT Policies and Firm Performance." *Accounting and Finance* 62 (1): 213–42.

Flores, A., D. Koehler, L. Lucchetti, C. Cortez, J. Djindjić, and L. Kuzmanov. 2023a. *The Economic Cost of Exclusion Based on Sexual Orientation, Gender Identity and Expression, and Sex Characteristics in the Labor Market in the Republic of North Macedonia.* Washington, DC: World Bank. http://hdl.handle.net/10986/40380.

Flores, A., D. Koehler, L. Lucchetti, C. Cortez, J. Djindjić, and L. Kuzmanov. 2023b. *The Economic Cost of Exclusion Based on Sexual Orientation, Gender Identity and Expression, and Sex Characteristics in the Labor Market in the Republic of Serbia.* Washington, DC: World Bank. http://hdl.handle.net/10986/40379.

Florida, R., and G. Gates. 2001. "Technology and Tolerance: The Importance of Diversity to High-Technology Growth." Center on Urban & Metropolitan Policy Survey Series, Brookings Institution, Washington, DC. https://www.brookings.edu/wp-content/uploads/2016/06/techtol.pdf.

FRA (Fundamental Rights Agency). 2020. *A Long Way to Go for LGBTI Equality.* EU-LGBT II. Luxembourg: Publications Office of the European Union. https://fra.europa.eu/en/publication/2020/eu-lgbti-survey-results.

Hafeez, H., M. Zeshan, M. A. Tahir, N. Jahan, and S. Naveed. 2017. "Health Care Disparities among Lesbian, Gay, Bisexual, and Transgender Youth: A Literature Review." *Cureus* 9 (4).

Haghighat, D., T. Berro, L. T. Sosa, K. Horowitz, B. Brown-King, and K. Zayhowski. 2023. "Intersex People's Perspectives on Affirming Healthcare Practices: A Qualitative Study." *Social Science and Medicine* 329 (9–10): 116047.

Heise, L., M. E. Greene, N. Opper, and M. Stavreopoulou. 2019. "Gender Inequality and Restrictive Gender Norms: Framing the Challenges to Health." *Lancet* 393 (10189): 2440–54.

Htun, M., F. Jensenius, and J. Nelson-Nuñez. 2019. "Gender-Discriminatory Laws and Women's Economic Agency." *Social Politics: International Studies in Gender, State, and Society* 26 (2): 193–222.

Human Rights Watch. 2016. "Shut Out: Restrictions on Bathroom and Locker Room Access for Transgender Youth in US Schools." Human Rights Watch. https://www.hrw.org/report/2016/09/15/shut-out/restrictions-bathroom-and-locker-room-access-transgender-youth-us.

Hyland, M., S. Djankov, and P. K. Goldberg. 2020. "Gendered Laws and Women in the Workforce." *AER Insights* 2 (4): 475–90.

Islam A., Muzi, S. and Amin, M. 2019. "Unequal Laws and the Disempowerment of Women in the Labour Market: Evidence from Firm-Level Data." *Journal of Development Studies* 55 (5): 822–44.

Khan, S., A. Bondyopadhyay, and K. Mulji. 2005. *From the Front Line: The Impact of Social, Legal and Judicial Impediments to Sexual Health Promotion and HIV and AIDS–Related Care and Support for Males Who Have Sex with Males in Bangladesh and India, a Study Report.* London, UK: Naz Foundation International.

Kosciw, J. G., C. M. Clark, and L. Menard. 2022. *The 2021 National School Climate Survey: The Experiences of LGBTQ+ Youth in Our Nation's Schools.* New York: GLSEN. https://www.glsen.org/sites/default/files/2022-10/NSCS-2021-Full-Report.pdf.

Li, F., and V. Nagar. 2013. "Diversity and Performance." *Management Science* 59 (3): 529–44.

Miller, J., and L. Parker. 2015. *Open for Business: The Economic and Business Case for Global LGB&T Inclusion.* Open for Business. https://diverzita.cz/wp-content/uploads/2016/11/Brunswick_Open_for_Business.pdf.

Noland, M. 2005. "Popular Attitudes, Globalization and Risk." 2005. *International Finance* 8 (2) (Summer 2005): 199–229.

Olivetti, C., and B. Petrongolo. 2017. "The Economic Consequences of Family Policies: Lessons from a Century of Legislation in High-Income Countries." *Journal of Economic Perspectives* 31 (1): 205–30.

O'Malley, J., and A. Holzinger. 2018. "Sustainable Development Goals: Sexual and Gender Minorities." United Nations Development Programme, New York. https://www.undp.org/publications/sexual-and-gender-minorities.

OECD (Organisation for Economic Co-operation and Development). 2020. *Over the Rainbow? The Road to LGBTI Inclusion.* Paris: OECD.

Equality of Opportunity for Sexual and Gender Minorities 2024

Pennings, S. 2020. "The Utilization-Adjusted Human Capital Index (UHCI)." Policy Research Working Paper 9375, World Bank, Washington, DC. https://documents1.worldbank.org/curated/en/630311600204533950/pdf/The-Utilization-adjusted-Human-Capital-Index-UHCI.pdf.

Rees-Turyn, A. M., C. Doyle, A. Holland, and S. Root. 2008. "Sexism and Sexual Prejudice (Homophobia): The Impact of the Gender Belief System and Inversion Theory on Sexual Orientation Research and Attitudes toward Sexual Minorities." *Journal of LGBT Issues in Counseling* 2 (1): 2–25.

Roy, S. 2019. "Discriminatory Laws against Women: A Survey of the Literature." Policy Research Working Paper 8719, World Bank, Washington, DC.

Sears, B., and C. Mallory. 2011. "Documented Evidence of Employment Discrimination and Its Effects on LGBT People." Williams Institute, UCLA School of Law, University of California at Los Angeles. https://escholarship.org/uc/item/03m1g5sg.

Sen, A. 1999. *Development as Freedom.* New York: Alfred Knopf. https://scholar.harvard.edu/sen/publications/development-freedom.

Sever, C. 2022. "Legal Gender Equality as a Catalyst for Convergence." IMF Working Paper No. 2022/155, International Monetary Fund, Washington, DC.

Shan, L., S. Fu, and L. Zheng. 2017. "Corporate Sexual Equality and Firm Performance." *Strategic Management Journal* 38: 1812–26.

UNDP (United Nations Development Programme). 2023. *Being LGBT in Jamaica National Survey for Lesbian, Gay, Bisexual, and Transgender Persons in Jamaica.* New York: UNDP. https://www.undp.org/latin-america/publications/being-lgbt-jamaica-national-survey-lesbian-gay-bisexual-and-transgender-persons-jamaica.

UNESCO (United Nations Educational, Scientific and Cultural Organization). 2012. *Education Sector Response to Homophobic Bullying.* Paris: UNESCO. https://unesdoc.unesco.org/ark:/48223/pf0000216493.

UNESCO (United Nations Educational, Scientific and Cultural Organization). 2015. *Out in the Open: Education Sector Responses to Violence Based on Sexual Orientation and Gender Identity/Expression.* Paris: UNESCO. unesdoc.unesco.org/images/0024/002447/244756e.pdf.

Vadlamannati, K., N. Janz, and Ø. I. Berntsen. 2018. "Human Rights Shaming and FDI: Effects of the UN Human Rights Commission and Council." *World Development* 104: 222–37.

Vu, T. V. 2021. "Does LGBT Inclusion Promote National Innovative Capacity?" Working paper, January 5, 2021. https://ssrn.com/abstract=3523553.

World Bank. 2011. *World Development Report 2012: Gender Equality and Development.* Washington, DC: World Bank.

World Bank. 2018. *Economic Inclusion of LGBTI Groups in Thailand: Main Report.* Washington, DC: World Bank. http://documents.worldbank.org/curated/en/269041521819512465/main-report.

World Bank. 2021. *The Human Capital Index 2020 Update: Human Capital in the Time of Covid-19.* Washington, DC: World Bank. https://openknowledge.worldbank.org/entities/publication/93f8fbc6-4513-58e7-82ec-af4636380319.

World Bank. 2022. *Social Cohesion and Forced Displacement: A Synthesis of New Research.* Washington, DC: World Bank. http://hdl.handle.net/10986/38431.

World Bank. 2023. *Women, Business and the Law 2023.* Washington, DC: World Bank.

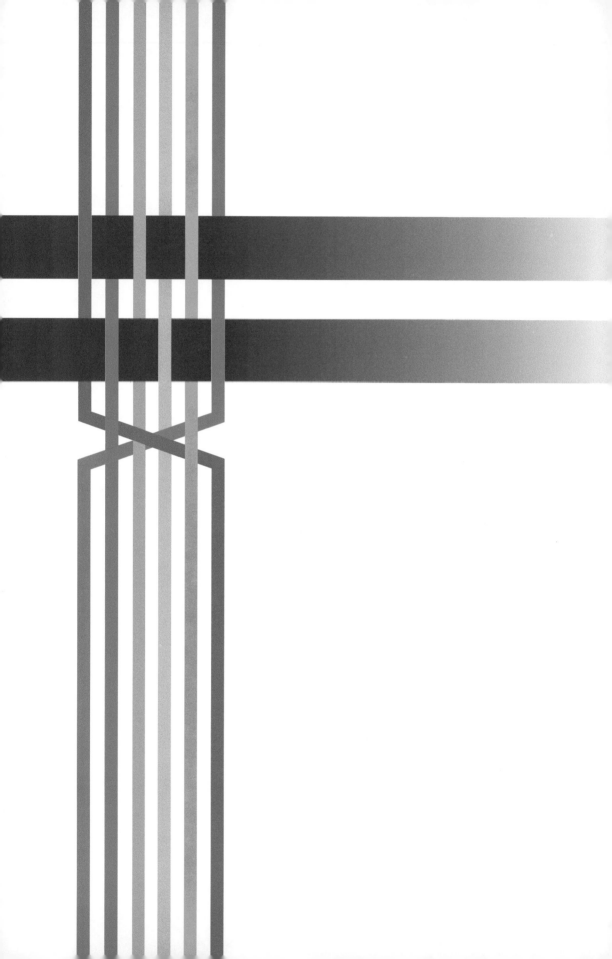

CHAPTER 4

Conclusions and the way forward

Lack of inclusive legal frameworks across all regions and groups

This report reveals large gaps in inclusive legal frameworks across the 64 countries covered by the Equality of Opportunity for Sexual and Gender Minorities (EQOSOGI) study. The average overall score is 0.31. More than half of the countries studied (35) have an overall EQOSOGI score of 0.30 or lower, suggesting a low presence of regulatory frameworks favoring the equality of opportunity for sexual and gender minorities. Over 40 percent of countries (26) exhibit a moderate presence of such legal, regulatory, and policy frameworks. Only three countries—Canada, France, and Spain—have an overall EQOSOGI score of 0.60 or higher and thus a high presence of inclusive regulatory frameworks.

For the three groups in this study—lesbian, gay, and bisexual (LGB); transgender; and intersex—equality of opportunity varies. Transgender people fare slightly better in terms of inclusive frameworks: the sample countries' overall score of 0.32 indicates that, on average, about 32 percent of the laws and policies suggested for promoting transgender peoples' inclusion are present across the sample countries. For LGB people, 30 percent of such laws and policies are present (a score of 0.30). Intersex people are the least covered by specific supportive legal and policy frameworks, with only 23 percent of suggested laws and policies present in the sample countries (a score of 0.23).

Regionally, the intersex group shows greater inclusion in the South Asia region but not in other regions. In Sub-Saharan Africa, the LGB group faces greater disadvantages than the intersex group. In the Middle East and North Africa, average EQOSOGI scores for LGB and intersex groups are almost identical, with both scoring lower than the transgender group.

A reproducibility package is available for this book in the Reproducible Research Repository at https://reproducibility.worldbank.org/index.php/catalog/182.

Progress in adopting inclusive legal and policy frameworks varies for each indicator set across regions. In all regions, scores are strongest in the Decriminalization indicator set, with the highest scores earned by the high-income Organisation for Economic Co-operation and Development countries (0.90), Europe and Central Asia (0.90), Latin America and the Caribbean (0.82), and East Asia and Pacific (0.75). Strong scores follow for Access to Services and Social Protection in the high-income Organisation for Economic Co-operation and Development countries, Latin America and the Caribbean, and South Asia, and for Civil and Political Inclusion in the high-income Organisation for Economic Co-operation and Development countries and in Latin America and the Caribbean. Regions score lower on Access to Education and Access to Labor Markets. Finally, Protection from Hate Crimes garners the weakest scores in all regions, with the Middle East and North Africa (0.01), East Asia and Pacific (0.02), South Asia (0.02), and Sub-Saharan Africa (0.03) scoring lowest. These scores indicate that, even in regions with relatively high levels of inclusion for some indicator sets such as Decriminalization, sexual and gender minorities continue to experience exclusion in other indicator sets, such as Access to Education, and weak protections from hate crimes and violence based on sexual orientation, gender identity and expression, and sex characteristics (SOGIESC). The Middle East and North Africa scores the lowest among all regions on all six indicator sets, highlighting significant gaps in SOGIESC inclusion in existing legal and policy frameworks in the region.

Inclusive and enabling legal and policy frameworks are fundamental to ensuring that all citizens can fully and effectively contribute to and benefit from a country's social and economic development. Lack of inclusive legal and policy frameworks systemically excludes individuals from efforts to improve human development and economic growth, so countries need to act quickly to ensure equality of opportunity for all.

Empirical findings on the association between EQOSOGI data and development outcomes focusing on wealth, human capital, voice and accountability, and income inequality highlight the importance of legal frameworks that promote equality of opportunity for sexual and gender minorities (refer to chapter 3). Wealthier countries tend to be more inclusive of sexual and gender minorities across all six indicator sets, with a statistically significant positive correlation between per capita real gross domestic product and overall EQOSOGI scores. The consistency of this pattern across all indicator sets suggests that economic prosperity is associated with greater inclusion of sexual and gender minorities. Higher levels of human capital and citizen's voice and accountability are also correlated with more inclusive environments for sexual and gender minorities, with statistically significant and positive correlations between EQOSOGI scores and the World Bank's Human Capital Index and Worldwide Governance Indicators estimates.[1]

Efforts toward greater SOGIESC inclusion

Since the September 2021 release of the first edition of this report, 5 of the 16 countries covered in the first edition have undertaken significant reforms aimed at fostering the inclusion and equal treatment under the law of people with diverse sexual orientation, gender identity and expression, and sex characteristics (box 4.1). These reforms include adopting SOGIESC action plans, introducing third gender options in official documents, and prohibiting "conversion therapies."

The World Bank has implemented several strategies and measures to ensure that the projects it funds, as well as its collaborations with partner countries, actively advance SOGIESC inclusivity and address the unique needs and challenges faced by SOGIESC communities (box 4.2).

BOX 4.1 Legal reforms related to inclusion of sexual and gender minorities in Canada, India, Japan, Kosovo, and Mexico since the first edition of EQOSOGI

Since the first edition of the *Equality of Opportunity for Sexual and Gender Minorities* (EQOSOGI) report, several countries have taken steps to promote inclusion of sexual and gender minorities. Of the 16 countries included in the first EQOSOGI, the following 5 have made significant reforms.

In January 2022, Canada enacted a new law that criminalized forcing or counseling someone to undergo "conversion therapy" and criminalized promoting or advertising "conversion therapy." Further, in August 2022, Canada launched its first Action Plan for advancing rights and equality for "Two-Spirit, lesbian, gay, bisexual, transgender, queer, intersex and additional people who identify as part of sexual and gender diverse communities."

In India, following a Madras High Court decision, the National Medical Council banned medical doctors' involvement in "conversion therapies." Although no national law exists against it, practicing such therapies is deemed illegal and constitutes professional misconduct under Indian Medical Council regulations, as of August 2022.

Additionally, in India, the state of Tamil Nadu has proposed a draft Gender and Sexual Minority (LGBTQIA+) policy that recommends several policy measures to foster social

(continued)

BOX 4.1 Legal reforms related to inclusion of sexual and gender minorities in Canada, India, Japan, Kosovo, and Mexico since the first edition of EQOSOGI *(continued)*

inclusion of sexual and gender minorities, including constituting a State Commission for Sexual and Gender Minorities.

India's Supreme Court also heard a case on the issue of marriage equality and legal recognition of same-sex marriages in the country. The court held that the right to marry is not a fundamental right but stated, however, that discrimination must end and urged parliament to decide upon same-sex marriage legislation.

In Japan, several courts have recently ruled in favor of sexual and gender minorities' rights. Nagoya and Sapporo district courts have ruled in favor of same-sex marriages and have declared unequal treatment of lesbian, gay, bisexual, transgender, and intersex people unconstitutional. In 2023, in a first ruling on the working environment for lesbian, gay, bisexual, transgender, and intersex people, the Japanese Supreme Court deemed it "unacceptable" to restrict a transgender woman's use of bathrooms at her workplace. However, these court rulings have not yet been translated into a comprehensive anti-discrimination law.

Kosovo's Program for Gender Equality 2020–2024 aims to prioritize gender equality in all aspects of Kosovo's transformation processes. It includes training for medical staff to ensure gender-sensitive services and equitable treatment for sexual and gender minorities.

Mexico's National Program for Equality and Nondiscrimination 2021–2024 (*Programa Nacional para la Igualdad y No Discriminación*, or Pronaind, established in December 2021) focuses on implementation of the government's antidiscrimination policy and aims to counter discriminatory practices, including those affecting sexual and gender minorities. Since 2021, Mexico has undertaken several steps toward effective legal gender recognition and civil and political inclusion of trans and gender diverse people. For example, in February 2023, the General Council of the National Electoral Institute approved incorporation of "X" as a third option for the gender marker in the Voter Identification Card. In May 2023, a passport application reform was announced, also allowing applicants to select "X" for the gender field.

Note: Data for the second edition of the EQOSOGI report are current as June 1, 2023.

BOX 4.2 The World Bank's efforts to mainstream SOGIESC inclusion

The World Bank is advancing sexual orientation, gender identity and expression, and sex characteristics (SOGIESC) inclusion through its commitment to gender equality, social inclusion, and nondiscrimination as outlined in the World Bank's Gender Strategy 2024–2030 (World Bank 2024), Social Sustainability and Inclusion Strategy, Environmental and Social Framework, and poverty reduction commitments.

The Sexual Orientation and Gender Identity team mainstreams SOGIESC inclusion across country programs by focusing on broadening the knowledge base, supporting operations, and building partnerships with internal and external stakeholders. It provides ad hoc and demand-driven technical support to Task Teams and clients, as well as training and capacity building to Task Teams and Country Management Units within the World Bank and Project Implementation Units within client governments. It also conducts consultations with SOGIESC-related civil society organizations to facilitate their input in the design and implementation of World Bank–funded operations.

To address the gaps in data on SOGIESC inclusion, the World Bank engages in a series of analytics and evidence-generation initiatives. In 2021, the World Bank produced the first edition of the research report *Equality of Opportunity for Sexual and Gender Minorities*, a first-of-its-kind analysis that benchmarks laws and regulations that either promote SOGIESC inclusion or create barriers to SOGIESC inclusion. In 2023, the World Bank conducted studies in North Macedonia and Serbia to measure the economic costs of exclusion by expanding the evidence base on SOGIESC-based exclusion in the labor market and estimating the economic and fiscal costs of exclusion of sexual and gender minorities (Flores et al. 2023a, 2023b).

Additionally, the Sexual Orientation and Gender Identity team works to develop expertise and good practice examples to showcase how SOGIESC inclusion can be operationalized effectively. The team has developed SOGIESC country profiles as well as technical notes to guide operations in select sectors, such as education and health.

These analytics and sector-specific technical notes aim to provide policy makers, civil society, and development partners with new evidence for the ongoing policy dialogue on strengthening the social inclusion of sexual and gender minorities; to complement and strengthen the discourse; and to facilitate positive change on these issues.

Areas for policy engagement to advance SOGIESC inclusion

1. **Improve data collection and analysis.** The lack of data on population numbers and lived experiences of sexual and gender minorities prevents solid analysis for economic and human development. Improved data in these areas can inform policy making and monitor progress toward inclusion. National censuses and other surveys should aim to collect and disaggregate data by sexual orientation, gender identity and expression, and sex characteristics as well as by the broader sex and gender categories, while guaranteeing the safety, privacy, and self-identification of sexual and gender minorities.

2. **Repeal criminalizing laws.** The first step to SOGIESC inclusion is to repeal criminalizing laws that enable systemic exclusion of sexual and gender minorities and put them at greater risk of harm and violence. Criminalization of SOGIESC-related activities perpetuates societal stigma and prejudice against sexual and gender minorities and poses barriers that prevent them from living a dignified life. Countries should repeal laws that criminalize same-sex activities between consenting adults (for example, laws against sodomy) and other laws that discriminate against sexual and gender minorities. These include laws that consider being a sexual or gender minority a mental or physical disorder (that is, pathologizing classifications that perpetuate myths and misconceptions about sexual and gender minorities being inherently ill) and laws that criminalize gender expression (for example, laws against "cross-dressing").

3. **Ensure legal gender recognition.** In the absence of legal gender recognition, transgender and intersex persons experience heightened levels of discrimination and lower levels of equality of opportunity. Targeted measures can contribute to ensuring nondiscrimination and inclusion for transgender and intersex persons, including laws and regulations that allow legal gender recognition on a self-identification basis without requiring medical interventions or lengthy administrative or judicial processes, that broaden binary gender categorizations, and that allow registration of intersex status at birth.

4. **Adopt laws to protect against violence and hate crimes.** Violence and hate crimes hinder equal participation of sexual and gender minorities, make them socially marginalized, and negatively affect economies and human capital. Countries should adopt legal and regulatory frameworks to combat SOGIESC-based violence and hate crimes, and harmful practices such as "conversion therapies" and irreversible, nonemergency medical surgeries on intersex children. Further, provision of appropriate training to health care providers and law enforcement officers can foster inclusive development.

5. **Enact inclusive legal frameworks.** Inclusion of sexual and gender minorities is likely to boost both economic and human development; conversely, SOGIESC-based exclusion negatively affects productivity and human capital (refer to chapter 3). Guaranteeing equal protection under the law across various sectors can promote inclusion. Countries should adopt legal and regulatory frameworks that protect sexual and gender minorities from discrimination in various sectors, guaranteeing them equal access to education, employment, and public services such as health care, housing, and social protection.

6. **Ensure freedom of association for sexual and gender minorities.** SOGIESC-related civil society groups are critical to assure full and meaningful participation of sexual and gender minorities. These civil society groups also play an important role in community outreach efforts and provision of services to the most marginalized and vulnerable sexual and gender minorities, including provision of health care services and support services to victims of violence. Countries should repeal laws and regulations that restrict freedom of association for sexual and gender minorities, and should abolish laws and policies that hamper the effective operations of SOGIESC-related civil society organizations to foster inclusive development efforts.

What's next?

The EQOSOGI team acknowledges the limitations of the current single-year data set in meeting the need for comparable cross-country data. The team is already conducting research to establish a data panel that will offer insights into legal and policy reforms over 50 years. Contingent on resources, the team intends to provide regular data updates on the EQOSOGI measurements, expanding the number of countries covered and the topics of the legal analysis, to include the following, for example.

: Disaggregation of the indicator sets into subgroups would allow analysis of intersectional experiences. For example, in analyzing the inclusion of LGB persons, a gender lens could be applied, separating the experience of lesbian and bisexual women from that of gay and bisexual men. Criminalization and lack of protection against discrimination may affect women disproportionately because of the gender bias prevalent in most societies (Human Dignity Trust 2016). In addition, separating sexual orientation from gender identity and expression and sex characteristics may fall short of capturing certain segments of the population—such as LGB transgender persons (Resiner et al. 2023) and LGB intersex persons. Furthermore, the data collected on transgender people in the countries covered conflate gender identity and expression, presenting an opportunity for future studies to disaggregate the two and the different forms of discrimination related to each.

- Given the importance of equal and inclusive access to health care for sexual and gender minorities, a separate chapter on health could provide more details about the barriers in accessing health care services.

- For transgender persons, the following issues, among others, could reveal a clearer picture of nondiscriminatory frameworks: whether a trans parent's gender identity is recognized on their child's birth certificate (Davis 2021); restrictive protocols for changing names in identity documents (Maier 2020); and the existence of public health insurance schemes providing coverage for trans-specific health care (Dowshen, Christensen, and Gruschow 2019).

- For access to services, future data collection may include issues such as regulation of access to bathrooms and extracurricular activities in schools based on gender identity (Human Rights Watch 2016); employment regulations on access to restrooms based on gender identity (Huffman et al. 2020); the availability of psychosocial services and medical care for victims of SOGIESC-based hate crimes (OSCE/ODIHR 2020); and the availability of assisted reproductive technology for trans persons. Future research could also explore affirmative action laws and SOGIESC-based regulations, including measures to guarantee access to private sector financing and to education and employment.

- Laws and regulations affecting private labor markets could be explored more comprehensively, mirroring public sector frameworks.

- Finally, because of the yawning gap in SOGIESC-specific data collection, further analysis may cover various forms of official surveys conducted to assess the lives of sexual and gender minorities.

Note

1. These correlations do not imply causality or indicate the direction of the relationship between development outcomes and EQOSOGI scores. Findings here are purely illustrative of the connections among education and skills, voice and accountability, and the environments supportive of sexual and gender minorities. This correlation is consistent across all indicator sets among the LGB, transgender, and intersex groups.

References

Davis, L. 2021. "Deconstructing Tradition: Trans Reproduction and the Need to Reform Birth Registration in England and Wales." *International Journal of Transgender Health* 22 (1–2): 179–90. doi: 10.1080/26895269.2020.1838394.

Dowshen, N. L., J. Christensen, and S. M. Gruschow. 2019. "Health Insurance Coverage of Recommended Gender-Affirming Health Care Services for Transgender Youth: Shopping Online for Coverage Information." *Transgender Health* 4 (1) (April 11): 131–35. doi: 10.1089/trgh.2019.0039.

Flores, A., D. Koehler, L. Lucchetti, C. Cortez, J. Djindjić, and L. Kuzmanov. 2023a. *The Economic Cost of Exclusion Based on Sexual Orientation, Gender Identity and Expression, and Sex Characteristics in the Labor Market in the Republic of North Macedonia.* Washington, DC: World Bank. http://hdl.handle.net/10986/40380.

Flores, A., D. Koehler, L. Lucchetti, C. Cortez, J. Djindjić, and L. Kuzmanov. 2023b. *The Economic Cost of Exclusion Based on Sexual Orientation, Gender Identity and Expression, and Sex Characteristics in the Labor Market in the Republic of Serbia.* Washington, DC: World Bank. http://hdl.handle.net/10986/40379.

Huffman, A. H., M. J. Mills, S. S. Howes, and M. D. Albritton. 2020. "Workplace Support and Affirming Behaviors: Moving toward a Transgender, Gender Diverse, and Non-binary Friendly Workplace." *International Journal of Transgender Health* 22 (3) (Dec. 21): 225-242. doi: 10.1080/26895269.2020.1861575.

Human Dignity Trust. 2016. "Breaking the Silence: Criminalisation of Lesbians and Bisexual Women and Its Impacts." Human Dignity Trust, London. https://www.humandignitytrust .org/wp-content/uploads/resources/Breaking-the-Silence-Criminalisation-of-LB-Women -and-its-Impacts-FINAL.pdf.

Human Rights Watch. 2016. "Shut Out: Restrictions on Bathroom and Locker Room Access for Transgender Youth in US Schools." Human Rights Watch. https://www.hrw.org/report/2016/09/15 /shut-out/restrictions-bathroom-and-locker-room-access-transgender-youth-us.

Maier, M. B. 2020. "Altering Gender Markers on Government Identity Documents: Unpredictable, Burdensome, and Oppressive." *University of Pennsylvania Journal of Law and Social Change* 203 (3): 203–50. https://scholarship.law.upenn.edu/jlasc/vol23/iss3/2/.

OSCE/ODIHR (Organization for Security and Co-operation in Europe/Office for Democratic Institutions and Human Rights). 2020. *Understanding the Needs of Hate Crime Victims.* Warsaw: OSCE/ODIHR. https://www.osce.org/files/f/documents/0/5/463011.pdf.

Resiner, S. L., S. K. Choi, J. L. Herman, W. Bockting, E. A. Krueger, and I. H. Meyer. 2023. "Sexual Orientation in Transgender Adults in the United States." *BMC Public Health* 23 (2023): 1–12. https://bmcpublichealth.biomedcentral.com/articles/10.1186/s12889-023-16654-z.

World Bank. 2024. *World Bank Group Gender Strategy 2024–2030: Accelerate Gender Equality to End Poverty on a Livable Planet.* Washington, DC: World Bank. http://documents.worldbank .org/curated/en/099061124182033630/BOSIB17e6952570c51b49812a89c05be6a4.

Glossary

The following terms provide a common basis for understanding concepts related to sexual orientation, gender identity and expression, and sex characteristics. Although these terms and definitions are presented here in the English language, the terms denoting sexual orientation and gender identity vary across cultures and languages. Therefore, this list is by no means complete or exhaustive.

Assisted reproductive technology (ART). All treatments or procedures that include the in vitro management of both human oocytes and sperm or embryos for establishing a pregnancy. These treatments or procedures include but are not limited to in vitro fertilization, embryo transfer, tubal embryo transfer, gamete and embryo cryopreservation, oocyte and embryo donation, and gestational surrogacy. ART does not include assisted insemination (artificial insemination) using sperm donation (Zegers-Hochschild et al. 2009).

Cisgender. A term used to refer to a person whose gender identity and expression correspond with the sex registered at birth (IESOGI 2017; UN 2016).

Cisnormativity. The belief that cisgender people and gender expressions are superior to trans, intersex, and nonbinary persons and expressions. The term is often used in conjunction with *heteronormativity* (UN Women 2022).

Conversion therapy. An umbrella term that describes wide-ranging interventions, all premised on the belief that a person's sexual orientation or gender identity, including *gender expression*, can and should be changed or suppressed when it does not conform with what other actors in a given setting and time perceive as the desirable norm—particularly when the person is lesbian, gay, bisexual, transgender, or *gender diverse* (IESOGI 2020).

Discrimination. Multiple and intersecting direct or indirect unequal or unfair treatment based on one or more grounds such as a person's age; sexual orientation, gender identity and expression, and sex characteristics; race; ethnicity; and religion (IESOGI 2017).

Gender-affirming health care. Any form of health care received by transgender and nonbinary people (refer to as *transgender or "trans"*) to align their body with their gender. Such care can include nonmedical care (such as hair removal, counseling support, mental health assessments, and voice therapy), medical care (such as gender-affirming hormone therapy and puberty blockers), and a wide range of gender-affirming surgeries (Coleman et al. 2022).

Gender-diverse. An umbrella term used to refer to persons whose gender identity, including their gender expression, does not conform to what is considered the norm at a particular time for the male/female gender binaries (IESOGI 2017).

Gender expression. A person's presentation of their gender by means of their physical appearance—including dress, hairstyle, accessories, and cosmetics—and mannerisms, speech, names, and personal pronouns. Gender expression may or may not conform with a person's *gender identity* (UN 2016).

Gender identity. A person's deeply felt internal and individual experience of gender (such as being a man, a woman, in between, neither, or something else), which may or may not correspond with the sex they were assigned at birth or the gender attributed to them by society. Gender identity can include a personal sense of body (which may involve, if freely chosen, modification of appearance or function by medical, surgical, or other means) and expressions of gender, including dress, speech, and mannerisms. Gender identity is not synonymous with *sexual orientation*. A person's internal gender identity is not necessarily visible to others (UN 2016).

Hate crimes. Offenses motivated by prejudice against a particular group of people. Prejudice could be based on such characteristics as race, ethnicity, religion, sexual orientation, gender identity and expression, and sex characteristics. Hate crime laws typically prohibit physical or verbal abuse against protected groups or the incitement of violence against them, or include penalty enhancement laws, such as an aggravating circumstance—for example, increasing the penalty for a basic crime when committed with a biased motive (Cortez, Arzinos, and De la Medina Soto 2021).

Heteronormativity. The belief that heterosexual individuals, behaviors, expressions, and relationships are superior to homosexual individuals, behaviors, expressions, and relationships (UN Women 2022).

Homophobia, transphobia, biphobia, intersex-phobia. The fear, hatred, or intolerance of homosexual people (homophobia), transgender people (transphobia), bisexual people (biphobia), or intersex people (intersex-phobia) as a social group or as individuals. These terms also describe discrimination and hate crimes based on sexual orientation, gender identity and expression, and sex characteristics (FRA 2011).

Intersex. An umbrella term that refers to people who have one or more of a range of variations in their biological sex characteristics that fall outside of traditional conceptions of male or female bodies. For some people, their intersex characteristics are identified at birth, whereas others may not discover their intersex traits until puberty or later in life. Intersex is not synonymous with *transgender* (OHCHR 2023).

Legal gender recognition. Laws, administrative procedures, or processes by which a person can change their legal sex/gender marker and name, for example, on official identity documents (refer to IESOGI 2018).

LGBTI. Lesbian, gay, bisexual, transgender, and/or intersex. Refer to *Sexual and gender minorities*.

Old-age benefits. Benefits for older persons that might include periodic pensions, subsidized long-term care, or transportation allowances (ILO 2021).

Pathologization. The psycho-medical, legal, and cultural practice of identifying a feature, an individual, or a population as intrinsically disordered. Transgender and intersex people (and lesbian, gay, and bisexual people in several countries) are often defined by medical authorities and institutions as inherently pathological (IESOGI 2018).

Pathologizing requirements. Transgender identity has been pathologized as a mental disorder or gender dysphoria in several countries across the world. In these country contexts, transgender persons are required to undergo a medical diagnosis as a precondition to receive gender-affirming hormonal treatment or surgeries. Pathologizing requirements discussed in this study refer to these diverse medical diagnosis conditions (IESOGI 2018).

Sex characteristics. Biological features related to sex, including genitalia, and other sexual and reproductive anatomy (OHCHR 2023).

Sexual and gender minorities. People whose sexual orientation, gender identity and gender expression, and/or sex characteristics differ from those of most of the society surrounding them. The term is often applied to lesbian, gay, bisexual, transgender, and/or intersex (LGBTI) people. Both LGBTI and LGBTQI+ are inclusive terms used to represent a range of orientations and identities, and the choice between these terms often depends on regional, cultural, or organizational preferences. This publication uses "LGBTI" and "sexual and gender minorities" for lesbian, gay, bisexual, transgender, and intersex persons, while recognizing other diverse sexual orientations and gender identities (IESOGI 2021; UN 2016).

Sexual orientation. A person's heterosexual, homosexual, bisexual, or other sexual or romantic orientation toward people of the same or different gender. An individual's sexual orientation is indicated by one or more of the following: (1) how a person identifies their sexual orientation; (2) a person's capacity for experiencing a sexual or romantic attraction to people of the same or different gender; or (3) a person's sexual or romantic behavior or relationship with a person of the same or different gender (refer to UN 2016).

Social protection. Policies and programs designed to reduce and prevent poverty, vulnerability, and social exclusion during the life cycle. Social protection interventions include a range of contributory interventions (such as social insurance) and noncontributory tax-financed benefits (ILO 2021).

SOGIESC. Sexual orientation, gender identity and expression, and sex characteristics.

Transgender or "trans." An umbrella term used to describe people whose gender identity differs from the sex they were assigned at birth. It encompasses trans men, trans women, and other gender-diverse people (OHCHR 2019). Not all gender-diverse people identify as transgender, nor will they necessarily use this term to describe themselves. In many economies, indigenous terms—such as *hijra, travesti,* and "two-spirit"—describe gender identities that are beyond the Western understanding of gender (UNDP and PGA 2022).

References

Coleman, E., A. E. Radix, W. P. Bouman, G. R. Brown, A. L. C. de Vries, M. B. Deutsch, R. Ettner, et al. 2022. "Standards of Care for the Health of Transgender and Gender Diverse People, Version 8." *International Journal of Transgender Health* 23 (Suppl. 1): S1–S259. doi: 10.1080/26895269.2022.2100644.

Cortez, C., J. Arzinos, and C. De la Medina Soto. 2021. *Equality of Opportunity for Sexual and Gender Minorities.* Washington, DC: World Bank. http://hdl.handle.net/10986/36288.

FRA (European Union Agency for Fundamental Rights). 2011. *Homophobia, Transphobia and Discrimination on Grounds of Sexual Orientation and Gender Identity in the EU Member States.* Vienna: FRA. https://fra.europa.eu/sites/default/files/fra _uploads/1659-FRA-homophobia-synthesis-report-2011_EN.pdf.

IESOGI (United Nations Independent Expert on Protection against Violence and Discrimination Based on Sexual Orientation and Gender Identity). 2017. "Report of the Independent Expert on Protection against Violence and Discrimination Based on Sexual Orientation and Gender Identity." A/HRC/35/1, Human Rights Council, thirty-fifth session, June 2017. https://digitallibrary.un.org/record/1301206?ln=en.

IESOGI (United Nations Independent Expert on Protection against Violence and Discrimination Based on Sexual Orientation and Gender Identity). 2018. "Report of the Independent Expert on Protection against Violence and Discrimination Based on Sexual Orientation and Gender Identity to the UN General Assembly." A/73/152. https://documents.un.org /doc/undoc/gen/n18/220/41/pdf/n1822041.pdf?token=s8IoF5Ii9LTrigXJj7&fe=true.

IESOGI (United Nations Independent Expert on Protection against Violence and Discrimination Based on Sexual Orientation and Gender Identity). 2020. "Practices of So-Called 'Conversion Therapy': Report of the Independent Expert on Protection against Violence

Glossary

and Discrimination Based on Sexual Orientation and Gender Identity." Report of the Special Procedure of the Human Rights Council, A/HRC/44/53. https://digitallibrary.un.org/record/3870697?ln=en&v=pdf#files.

IESOGI (United Nations Independent Expert on Protection against Violence and Discrimination Based on Sexual Orientation and Gender Identity). 2021. "The Law of Inclusion: Report of the Independent Expert on Sexual Orientation and Gender Identity," A/HRC/47/27. https://www.ohchr.org/en/documents/thematic-reports/ahrc4727-law-inclusion-report-independent-expert-sexual-orientation-and.

ILO (International Labour Organization). 2021. *World Social Protection Report 2020–22: Social Protection at the Crossroads: In Pursuit of a Better Future*. Geneva: ILO. https://www.ilo.org/wcmsp5/groups/public/@ed_protect/@soc_sec/documents/publication/wcms_817572.pdf.

OHCHR (Office of the United Nations High Commissioner for Human Rights). 2019. "The Right to Housing of LGBT Youth: An Urgent Task in the SDG Agenda Setting." Statement, Special Procedures, OHCHR, New York.

OHCHR (Office of the United Nations High Commissioner for Human Rights). 2023. "Technical Note on the Human Rights of Intersex People: Human Rights Standards and Good Practices." OHCHR, New York. https://www.ohchr.org/sites/default/files/2023-11/ohchr-technical-note-rights-intersex-people.pdf.

UN (United Nations). 2016. "Living Free & Equal: What States are Doing to Tackle Violence and Discrimination against Lesbian, Gay, Bisexual, Transgender and Intersex People." UN, New York and Geneva. https://www.ohchr.org/sites/default/files/Documents/Publications/LivingFreeAndEqual.pdf.

UNDP (United Nations Development Programme) and PGA (Parliamentarians for Global Action). 2022. "Advancing the Human Rights and Inclusion of LGBTI People: A Handbook for Parliamentarians." UNDP, New York. https://www.undp.org/sites/g/files/zskgke326/files/2023-04/Advancing%20the%20human%20rights%20of%20LGBTI%20people%20-%20ENGLISH.pdf.

UN Women. 2022. "LGBTIQ+ Equality and Rights: Internal Resource Guide." UN Women, New York. https://www.unwomen.org/en/digital-library/publications/2022/06/lgbtiq-equality-and-rights-internal-resource-guide.

Zegers-Hochschild, F., G. D. Adamson, J. de Mouzon, O. Ishihara, R. Mansour, K. Nygren, E. Sullivan, and S. Vanderpoel. 2009. "International Committee for Monitoring Assisted Reproductive Technology (ICMART) and the World Health Organization (WHO) Revised Glossary of ART Terminology, 2009." *Fertility and Sterility* 92 (5) (November 2009): 1520–24. https://www.fertstert.org/article/S0015-0282(09)03688-7/fulltext.

Appendixes

Appendix A provides a comprehensive list of questions used for the study across all indicator sets and the coding methodology. It includes the 138 questions (plus 10 additional unscored questions) used for *Equality of Opportunity for Sexual and Gender Minorities 2024* (EQOSOGI). Appendix B contains the scoring methodology and details on how it is constructed, including the steps for developing the EQOSOGI score, which involves the coding of legal responses into a binary quantitative indicator, quality control of these indicators, and computation of the indicator set scores and the EQOSOGI score. Appendix C includes the names of local experts and organizations wishing to be acknowledged individually from the 64 countries that participated in the study. There are also online-only appendixes that include the EQOSOGI codebook, data set, descriptive statistics, EQOSOGI overall and indicator set scores summary statistics, overall score, indicator set scores, and scores by SOGIESC group. You can access the online appendixes by scanning the QR code below.

A reproducibility package is available for this book in the Reproducible Research Repository at https://reproducibility.worldbank.org/index.php/catalog/182.

Appendix A
Questions and coding methodology

This appendix shows the 138 questions used for the 2024 EQOSOGI report (plus 10 additional unscored questions). Analysis for this report considers only laws, regulations, and policies in place as of June 1, 2023. Refer to appendix B for the scoring methodology.

1. Decriminalization

1.1. Do any laws or regulations explicitly criminalize people based on their diverse sexual orientation, gender identity and expression, and sex characteristics (SOGIESC)?

• 1.1a. Sexual orientation	Yes = 0; No = 1
• 1.1b. Gender identity and expression	Yes = 0; No = 1
• 1.1c. Sex characteristics (intersex persons)	Yes = 0; No = 1

Answer "Yes" if an explicit legal provision criminalizes people on the basis of their diverse SOGIESC, or if there is evidence, such as a higher court decision, that legal provisions are used to criminalize same-sex sexual activities or gender identity and expression or intersex people.

Answer "No" if there is no such provision.

1.2. Are same-sex relations between consenting adults explicitly criminalized?

	Yes = 0; No = 1

Answer "Yes" if an explicit legal provision criminalizes same-sex relations between consenting adults.

Answer "No" if there is no such provision.

1.3. Is the legal age for consensual sex for heterosexuals and for sexual and gender minorities the same? Yes = 0; No = 1; N/A = 0

Answer "Yes" if the legal provision setting the legal age for consensual sex does not differentiate between sexual and gender minorities and heterosexuals.

Answer "No" if a legal provision setting a legal age for consensual sex for sexual and gender minorities differs from that for heterosexuals.

Answer "Not applicable" (N/A) if same-sex relations between consenting adults are criminalized.

1.4. Are sexual and gender minorities targeted with other laws such as vagrancy, public nuisance, or public morals?

- 1.4a. Sexual orientation   Yes = 0; No = 1
- 1.4b. Gender identity and expression   Yes = 0; No = 1
- 1.4c. Sex characteristics (intersex persons)   Yes = 0; No = 1

Answer "Yes" if laws or regulations on vagrancy, public nuisance, or morals are used by prosecutors and courts to target people on the basis of their diverse SOGIESC.

Answer "No" if there is no record of such laws being used.

1.5. Do any laws or regulations call for transgender and intersex people who have been convicted of a crime to be incarcerated in correctional facilities, jails, and prisons according to their gender identity and expression or sex characteristics? Yes = 1; No = 0

Answer "Yes" if an explicit legal provision calls for transgender and intersex people who have been convicted of a crime to be incarcerated in correctional facilities, jails, and prisons according to their gender identity and expression or sex characteristics.

Answer "No" if there is no such provision.

1.6. Do any laws or regulations prohibit persons from freely expressing their gender expressions—for example, laws against "cross-dressing"? Yes = 0; No = 1

Answer "Yes" if an explicit legal provision prohibits persons from freely expressing their gender expressions.

Answer "No" if there is no such provision.

2. Access to education

2.1. Do any laws, constitutional provisions, or regulations prohibit discrimination against students or teachers in educational settings based on SOGIESC?

- 2.1a. Sexual orientation   Yes = 1; No = 0
- 2.1b. Gender identity and expression   Yes = 1; No = 0
- 2.1c. Sex characteristics (intersex persons)   Yes = 1; No = 0

Answer "Yes" if there is an explicit legal protection from discrimination in educational settings based on diverse SOGIESC.

Answer "No" if there is a generic legal protection from discrimination in education, or if there is no legal protection at all.

2.2. Do any laws or regulations prohibit discrimination in school admissions based on SOGIESC?

- 2.2a. Sexual orientation   Yes = 1; No = 0
- 2.2b. Gender identity and expression   Yes = 1; No = 0
- 2.2c. Sex characteristics (intersex persons)   Yes = 1; No = 0

Answer "Yes" if there is an explicit legal protection from discrimination in school admissions based on diverse SOGIESC.

Answer "No" if there is a generic legal protection from discrimination in school admissions, or if there is no legal protection at all.

2.3. Do any laws or regulations that prohibit bullying, cyberbullying, and harassment of students or teachers in the educational system include students based on actual or perceived SOGIESC?

- 2.3a. Sexual orientation   Yes = 1; No = 0
- 2.3b. Gender identity and expression   Yes = 1; No = 0
- 2.3c. Sex characteristics (intersex persons)   Yes = 1; No = 0

Answer "Yes" if there is an explicit legal protection from bullying, cyberbullying, or harassment in the educational system based on diverse SOGIESC.

Answer "No" if there is a generic legal protection from bullying, cyberbullying, and harassment in the educational system, or if there is no legal protection at all.

2.4. Do any laws or regulations mandate the revision of national textbooks or national curricula in primary and secondary education to eliminate discriminatory language (such as homophobic, transphobic, or intersex-phobic) or to add gender-inclusive and nonheteronormative language (such as replacing "boys and girls" with "students" and "mom and dad" with "family" or "caring adult" and normalizing the use of preferred pronouns)? Yes ≡ 1; No ≡ 0

Answer "Yes" if an explicit legal provision mandates the revision of national textbooks or national curricula in primary and secondary education to eliminate discriminatory language based on SOGIESC or to add gender-inclusive and nonheteronormative language.

Answer "No" if there is no such provision.

2.5. Do any laws or regulations mandate training teachers and other school staff in primary and secondary education with the objective of preventing discrimination against students who are sexual or gender minorities or have atypical sex characteristics (or intersex people) or who are perceived as such? Yes ≡ 1; No ≡ 0

Answer "Yes" if an explicit legal provision mandates training of teachers and other school staff in primary and secondary education with the objective of preventing discrimination against students who are sexual or gender minorities or who are perceived as such.

Answer "No" if there is no such provision.

2.6. Do any laws or regulations mandate the creation of courses on sex education in a SOGIESC-inclusive manner in secondary and tertiary education? Yes ≡ 1; No ≡ 0

Answer "Yes" if an explicit legal provision mandates the creation of courses on sex education in a SOGIESC-inclusive manner in secondary and tertiary education.

Answer "No" if there is no such provision.

2.7. Are there any concrete mechanisms (national or local) for reporting SOGIESC-related discrimination, violence, bullying, or cyberbullying directed at students, including incidents perpetrated by representatives of the education sector such as teachers and other school staff? Yes ≡ 1; No ≡ 0

Answer "Yes" if an explicit legal provision introduces concrete mechanisms for reporting cases of SOGIESC-related discrimination, violence, bullying, or cyberbullying directed at students.

Answer "No" if there is no such provision.

Appendix A: Questions and coding methodology

2.8. Do any laws and or regulations prohibit students from dressing or expressing themselves in accordance with their gender identities? Yes = 0; No = 1

Yes = 0; No = 1

Answer "Yes" if an explicit legal provision prohibits students from dressing or expressing themselves in accordance with their gender identities.

Answer "No" if there is no such provision.

Answer "Yes" if an explicit legal provision prohibits students from dressing or expressing themselves in accordance with their gender identities.

Answer "No" if there is no such provision.

2. Access to education

109

3. Acess to labor markets

3.1. Do any laws, constitutional provisions, or regulations prohibit discrimination based on diverse SOGIESC in public and private sector workplaces?

3.1.1. Public sector

- 3.1.1a. Sexual orientation   Yes = 1; No = 0
- 3.1.1b. Gender identity and expression   Yes = 1; No = 0
- 3.1.1c. Sex characteristics (intersex persons) Yes = 1; No = 0

Answer "Yes" if there is an explicit legal protection from discrimination based on diverse SOGIESC in public sector workplaces at the federal level.

Answer "No" if there is a generic legal protection from discrimination in public sector workplaces, or if there is no legal protection at all.

3.1.2. Private sector

- 3.1.2a. Sexual orientation   Yes = 1; No = 0
- 3.1.2b. Gender identity and expression   Yes = 1; No = 0
- 3.1.2c. Sex characteristics (intersex persons) Yes = 1; No = 0

Answer "Yes" if there is an explicit legal protection from discrimination based on diverse SOGIESC in private sector workplaces at the national level.

Answer "No" if there is a generic legal protection from discrimination in private sector workplaces, or if there is no legal protection at all.

3.2. Do any laws or regulations prohibit discrimination in recruitment in the public and private sectors based on diverse SOGIESC?

3.2.1. Public sector

- 3.2.1a. Sexual orientation   Yes = 1; No = 0
- 3.2.1b. Gender identity and expression   Yes = 1; No = 0
- 3.2.1c. Sex characteristics (intersex persons) Yes = 1; No = 0

Answer "Yes" if there is an explicit legal protection from discrimination based on diverse SOGIESC in recruitment in the public sector.

Answer "No" if there is a generic legal protection from discrimination in public sector workplaces, or if there is no legal protection at all.

3.2.2. Private sector

- 3.2.2a. Sexual orientation   Yes = 1; No = 0
- 3.2.2b. Gender identity and expression   Yes = 1; No = 0
- 3.2.2c. Sex characteristics (intersex persons)   Yes = 1; No = 0

Answer "Yes" if there is an explicit legal protection from discrimination based on diverse SOGIESC in recruitment in the private sector.

Answer "No" if there is a generic legal protection from discrimination in private sector workplaces, or if there is no legal protection at all.

3.3. Do any laws or regulations prohibit an employer from asking about an individual's SOGIESC during the recruitment process?

- 3.3a. Sexual orientation   Yes = 1; No = 0
- 3.3b. Gender identity and expression   Yes = 1; No = 0
- 3.3c. Sex characteristics (intersex persons)   Yes = 1; No = 0

Answer "Yes" if an explicit legal provision prohibits an employer from asking about an individual's SOGIESC during the recruitment process.

Answer "No" if there is no such legal provision at all.

3.4. Do any laws, constitutional provisions, or regulations prescribe equal remuneration for work of equal value for sexual and gender minorities?

- 3.4a. Sexual orientation   Yes = 1; No = 0
- 3.4b. Gender identity and expression   Yes = 1; No = 0
- 3.4c. Sex characteristics (intersex persons)   Yes = 1; No = 0

Answer "Yes" if an explicit legal provision prescribes equal remuneration for work of equal value for people with diverse SOGIESC.

Answer "No" if there is no such legal provision at all.

3.5. Do any laws or regulations prohibit the dismissal of employees on the basis of their perceived or actual SOGIESC?

- 3.5a. Sexual orientation   Yes = 1; No = 0
- 3.5b. Gender identity and expression   Yes = 1; No = 0
- 3.5c. Sex characteristics (intersex persons)   Yes = 1; No = 0

Answer "Yes" if an explicit legal provision prohibits the dismissal of employees based on SOGIESC.

Answer "No" if there is no such legal provision at all.

3.6. Do any laws or regulations allow an employee to bring a claim for employment discrimination on SOGIESC grounds in the public and private sectors?

3.6.1. Public sector

- 3.6.1a. Sexual orientation
- 3.6.1a. Sexual orientation
- 3.6.1b. Gender identity and expression
- 3.6.1b. Gender identity and expression
- 3.6.1c. Sex characteristics (intersex persons)
- 3.6.1c. Sex characteristics (intersex persons)

Yes ≡ 1; No ≡ 0
Yes ≡ 1; No ≡ 0
Yes ≡ 1; No ≡ 0

Answer "Yes" if an explicit legal provision allows an employee to bring a claim for employment discrimination based on SOGIESC in the public sector.

Answer "No" if there is no such legal provision at all.

3.6.2. Private sector

- 3.6.2a. Sexual orientation
- 3.6.2a. Sexual orientation
- 3.6.2b. Gender identity and expression
- 3.6.2b. Gender identity and expression
- 3.6.2c. Sex characteristics (intersex persons)
- 3.6.2c. Sex characteristics (intersex persons)

Yes ≡ 1; No ≡ 0
Yes ≡ 1; No ≡ 0
Yes ≡ 1; No ≡ 0

Answer "Yes" if an explicit legal provision allows an employee to bring a claim for employment discrimination based on SOGIESC in the private sector.

Answer "No" if there is no such legal provision at all.

3.7. Does a national equality body or national human rights institution have an explicit mandate to handle charges of employment discrimination related to diverse SOGIESC?

- 3.7a. Sexual orientation
- 3.7a. Sexual orientation
- 3.7b. Gender identity and expression
- 3.7b. Gender identity and expression
- 3.7c. Sex characteristics (intersex persons)
- 3.7c. Sex characteristics (intersex persons)

Yes ≡ 1; No ≡ 0
Yes ≡ 1; No ≡ 0
Yes ≡ 1; No ≡ 0

Answer "Yes" if an explicit legal provision mandates a national equality body or national human rights institution to handle charges of employment discrimination related to diverse SOGIESC.

Answer "No" if there is no such legal provision at all.

3.8. Does the pension system provide the same benefits to same-sex partners and different-sex spouses?

3.8.1. Public sector

Yes ≡ 1; No ≡ 0

Answer "Yes" if an explicit legal provision prescribes that the pension system in the public sector provide the same benefits to same-sex partners and different-sex spouses.

Answer "No" if there is no such legal provision, or if the pension system does not cover same-sex partners.

3.8.2. Private sector Yes = 1; No = 0

Answer "Yes" if an explicit legal provision prescribes that the pension system in the private sector provide the same benefits to same-sex partners and different-sex spouses.

Answer "No" if there is no such legal provision, or if the pension system does not cover same-sex partners.

3.9. Do any laws or regulations require workplaces to have inclusive facilities, such as gender-neutral toilets? Yes = 1; No = 0

Answer "Yes" if an explicit legal provision requires workplaces to have inclusive facilities, such as gender-neutral toilets.

Answer "No" if there is no such legal provision.

3.10. Do any laws or regulations prohibit employees from dressing or expressing themselves in accordance with their gender identities? Yes = 0; No = 1

Answer "Yes" if an explicit legal provision prohibits employees from dressing or expressing themselves in accordance with their gender identities.

Answer "No" if there is no such legal provision.

4. Access to services and social protection

4.1. Do any laws, constitutional provisions, or regulations explicitly prohibit discrimination based on SOGIESC in accessing any of the following services?

4.1.1. Health care

- 4.1.1a. Sexual orientation   Yes = 1; No = 0
- 4.1.1b. Gender identity and expression   Yes = 1; No = 0
- 4.1.1c. Sex characteristics (intersex persons)   Yes = 1; No = 0

Answer "Yes" if any laws, constitutional provisions, or regulations explicitly prohibit discrimination in health care services based on SOGIESC.

Answer "No" if no laws, constitutional provisions, or regulations explicitly prohibit discrimination in health care services based on SOGIESC.

4.1.2. Housing

- 4.1.2a. Sexual orientation   Yes = 1; No = 0
- 4.1.2b. Gender identity and expression   Yes = 1; No = 0
- 4.1.2c. Sex characteristics (intersex persons)   Yes = 1; No = 0

Answer "Yes" if any laws, constitutional provisions, or regulations explicitly prohibit discrimination in housing services based on SOGIESC.

Answer "No" if no laws, constitutional provisions, or regulations explicitly prohibit discrimination in housing services based on SOGIESC.

4.1.3. Social protection or other services (such as benefits related to unemployment, pension, disability, transportation, low-income families)

- 4.1.3a. Sexual orientation   Yes = 1; No = 0
- 4.1.3b. Gender identity and expression   Yes = 1; No = 0
- 4.1.3c. Sex characteristics (intersex persons)   Yes = 1; No = 0

Answer "Yes" if any laws, constitutional provisions, or regulations explicitly prohibit discrimination in social protection or other services based on SOGIESC.

Answer "No" if no laws, constitutional provisions, or regulations explicitly prohibit discrimination in social protection or other services based on SOGIESC.

4.2. Does the public health insurance scheme provide same-sex partners and different-sex partners with equal benefits? Yes = 1; No = 0

Answer "Yes" if the public health insurance scheme provides same-sex partners and different-sex partners with equal benefits.

Answer "No" if the public health insurance scheme does not provide same-sex partners and different-sex partners with equal benefits.

4.3. Does the national census include questions on the SOGIESC status of individuals?
- 4.3a. Sexual orientation Yes = 1; No = 0
- 4.3b. Gender identity and expression Yes = 1; No = 0
- 4.3c. Sex characteristics (intersex persons) Yes = 1; No = 0

Answer "Yes" if the national census (or primary statistical instrument to count the population and its characteristics in the country) includes questions on the population's SOGIESC.

Answer "No" if the national census (or primary statistical instrument) does not include questions on the population's SOGIESC.

Answer "No" if the national census (or primary statistical instrument) does not include questions on the population's SOGIESC, but instead a separate household or social survey is conducted to measure the relevant data.

4.4. Are civil society organizations (CSOs) related to sexual minority rights, transgender rights, or intersex rights permitted to operate in the country?
- 4.4a. Sexual minority rights Yes = 1; No = 0
- 4.4b. Transgender rights Yes = 1; No = 0
- 4.4c. Intersex rights Yes = 1; No = 0

Answer "Yes" if CSOs related to sexual minority rights, transgender rights, or intersex rights are allowed to register and openly operate in the country.

Answer "No" if CSOs related to sexual minority rights, transgender rights, or intersex rights are not allowed to register or do not openly operate in the country.

4.5. If "Yes," are CSOs subject to limitation by the state based on national security, public order, morality, or other grounds?
- 4.5a. Sexual minority rights Yes = 0; No = 1, N/A = 0
- 4.5b. Transgender rights Yes = 0; No = 1, N/A = 0
- 4.5c. Intersex rights Yes = 0; No = 1, N/A = 0

Equality of Opportunity for Sexual and Gender Minorities 2024

Answer "Yes" if CSOs related to sexual minority rights, transgender rights, or intersex rights are subject to limitation by the state based on national security, public order, morality, or other grounds.

Answer "No" if CSOs related to sexual minority rights, transgender rights, or intersex rights are not subject to limitation by the state based on national security, public order, morality, or other grounds.

Answer "Not applicable" (N/A) if CSOs related to sexual minority rights, transgender rights, or intersex rights are not permitted in the country.

4.6. Do any laws or regulations prohibit CSOs from providing social services specifically to sexual and gender minorities? Examples are vaccination, sanitation, transportation, family planning, health services (psychological, physiological, and sexual and reproductive), HIV preventive services (such as condoms, lubricants, preexposure prophylaxis), and information on vulnerable sexual practices, antiretrovirals, medication for gender-reassignment surgery, and support for transgender people during and after gender-reassignment surgery?

- 4.6a. Sexual orientation — Yes ≡ 0; No ≡ 1
- 4.6b. Gender identity and expression — Yes ≡ 0; No ≡ 1
- 4.6c. Sex characteristics (intersex persons) — Yes ≡ 0; No ≡ 1

Answer "Yes" if any laws or regulations prohibit CSOs from providing social services specifically to persons with diverse SOGIESC.

Answer "No" if no laws or regulations prohibit CSOs from providing social services specifically to persons with diverse SOGIESC.

4.7. Do any laws or regulations impose funding limitations on CSOs for the provision of such services?

- 4.7a. Sexual orientation — Yes ≡ 0; No ≡ 1
- 4.7b. Gender identity and expression — Yes ≡ 0; No ≡ 1
- 4.7c. Sex characteristics (intersex persons) — Yes ≡ 0; No ≡ 1

Answer "Yes" if any laws or regulations impose funding limitations on CSOs on providing such services to persons with diverse SOGIESC.

Answer "No" if no laws or regulations impose funding limitations on CSOs on providing such services to persons with diverse SOGIESC.

4.8. Do any laws or regulations establish national human rights institutions (NHRIs) that include diverse SOGIESC in their mandate or specific institutions with an explicit mandate to advance the inclusion of people with diverse SOGIESC?

- 4.8a. Sexual orientation — Yes = 1; No = 0
- 4.8b. Gender identity and expression — Yes = 1; No = 0
- 4.8c. Sex characteristics (intersex persons) — Yes = 1; No = 0

Answer "Yes" if specific provisions include diverse SOGIESC or advance the inclusion of persons with diverse SOGIESC in the mandate of NHRIs or a national equality body.

Answer "No" if no specific provisions include diverse SOGIESC or advance the inclusion of persons with diverse SOGIESC in the mandate of NHRIs or a national equality body.

4.9. Does a national equality body or NHRI handle charges of SOGIESC-based discrimination in public services?

- 4.9a. Sexual orientation — Yes = 1; No = 0
- 4.9b. Gender identity and expression — Yes = 1; No = 0
- 4.9c. Sex characteristics (intersex persons) — Yes = 1; No = 0

Answer "Yes" if the NHRI or national equality body has an explicit mandate to handle charges of discrimination in public services based on SOGIESC.

Answer "No" if the NHRI or national equality body does not have an explicit mandate to handle charges of discrimination in public services based on SOGIESC.

4.10. Do applications for identification (ID) cards or passports offer only two options: male or female?

- 4.10a. ID card — Yes = 0; No = 1
- 4.10b. Passport — Yes = 0; No = 1

Answer "Yes" if ID card or passport applications offer only two options: male or female.

Answer "No" if ID card or passport applications offer at least one other option in addition to male or female.

4.11. Does the law allow parents to register the birth of a child without a specified gender or as intersex? — Yes = 1; No = 0

Answer "Yes" if the law allows parents to register the birth of a child without a specified gender or as intersex.

Answer "No" if the law requires parents to register the birth of a child with a specified gender.

4. Access to services and social protection

4.12. Do any laws or regulations allow an individual to obtain a new ID card or passport after gender reassignment? Yes = 1; No = 0

Answer "Yes" if any laws or regulations allow an individual to obtain a new ID card or passport after gender reassignment (including but not limited to medical gender reassignment surgery).

Answer "No" if laws or regulations do not allow an individual to obtain a new ID card or passport after gender reassignment.

4.13. Do any laws or regulations allow for updating sex/gender in ID cards and/or passports based on self-declared gender identity? Yes = 1; No = 0

Answer "Yes" if laws or regulations allow for updating sex/gender in ID cards and/or passports based on self-declared gender identity without requiring medical certificates, psychiatric assessments, or other pathologizing requirements.

Answer "No" if laws or regulations do not allow for updating sex/gender in ID cards and/or passports based on self-declared gender identity; or if laws or regulations do not allow an individual to obtain a new ID card or passport after gender reassignment.

4.14. Do any laws or regulations prevent sexual and gender minorities and people with sex characteristics variations (intersex) or same-sex partners from donating blood? Yes = 0; No = 1

Answer "Yes" if any laws or regulations prevent sexual and gender minorities and people with sex characteristics variations (intersex) or same-sex partners from donating blood.

Answer "No" if no laws or regulations prevent sexual and gender minorities and people with sex characteristics variations (intersex) or same-sex partners from donating blood.

5. Civil and political inclusion

5.1. Do any members of parliament or other national elected representative body currently openly self-identify as a sexual or gender minority or as intersex?

Yes = 1; No = 0

Answer "Yes" if any members of parliament or other national elected representative body currently openly self-identify as a sexual or gender minority or as intersex.

Answer "No" if no members of parliament or other national elected representative body currently openly self-identify as a sexual or gender minority or as intersex.

5.2. Do any members of the cabinet or the executive branch currently openly self-identify as a sexual or gender minority or as intersex? Yes = 1; No = 0

Answer "Yes" if any members of the cabinet or the executive branch currently openly self-identify as a sexual or gender minority or as intersex.

Answer "No" if no members of the cabinet or the executive branch currently openly self-identify as a sexual or gender minority or as intersex.

5.3. Do any members of the supreme court or other highest court currently openly self-identify as a sexual or gender minority or as intersex? Yes = 1; No = 0

Answer "Yes" if any members of the supreme court or other highest court currently openly self-identify as a sexual or gender minority or as intersex.

Answer "No" if no members of the supreme court or other highest court currently openly self-identify as a sexual or gender minority or as intersex.

5.4. Is there a national action plan on the issues of persons with diverse SOGIESC?
- 5.4a. Sexual orientation   Yes = 1; No = 0
- 5.4b. Gender identity and expression   Yes = 1; No = 0
- 5.4c. Sex characteristics (intersex persons)   Yes = 1; No = 0

Answer "Yes" if there is a national action plan on the issues of persons with diverse SOGIESC.

Answer "No" if there is no national action plan on the issues of persons with diverse SOGIESC.

5.5. Do any laws or regulations restrict the expression, civic participation, or association of people with diverse SOGIESC?

- 5.4a. Sexual orientation — Yes ≡ 0; No ≡ 1
- 5.4b. Gender identity and expression — Yes ≡ 0; No ≡ 1
- 5.4c. Sex characteristics (intersex persons) — Yes ≡ 0; No ≡ 1

Answer "Yes" if any laws or regulations restrict the expression, civic participation, or association of people with diverse SOGIESC.

Answer "No" if no laws or regulations restrict the expression, civic participation, or association of people with diverse SOGIESC.

5.6. Can same-sex couples enter into a registered partnership or civil union?

Yes ≡ 1; No ≡ 0

Answer "Yes" if same-sex couples are allowed to enter into a registered partnership or civil union.

Answer "No" if same-sex couples are not allowed to enter into a registered partnership or civil union.

5.7. Can same-sex couples marry legally?

Yes ≡ 1; No ≡ 0

Answer "Yes" if same-sex couples are allowed to marry legally.

Answer "No" if same-sex couples are not allowed to marry legally.

5.8. Does the law consider registered partnerships or civil unions entered into by same-sex partners in other countries valid?

Yes ≡ 1; No ≡ 0

Answer "Yes" if same-sex partnerships or civil unions entered into by same-sex partners in other countries are recognized legally.

Answer "No" if same-sex partnerships or civil unions entered into by same-sex partners in other countries are not recognized legally.

5.9. Does the law consider legal marriages entered into by same-sex partners in other countries valid?

Yes ≡ 1; No ≡ 0

Answer "Yes" if same-sex marriages entered into by same-sex partners in other countries are recognized legally.

Answer "No" if same-sex marriages entered into by same-sex partners in other countries are not recognized legally.

Appendix A: Questions and coding methodology

5.10. Is second parent or joint adoption by same-sex partner(s) legally possible?

Yes = 1; No = 0
Yes = 1; No = 0

Answer "Yes" if second parent or joint adoption by same-sex partner(s) is legally possible.

Answer "No" if second parent or joint adoption by same-sex partner(s) is not legally possible.

5.11. Do any laws or regulations grant different-sex and same-sex couples equal access to assisted reproductive technology?

Yes = 1; No = 0
Yes = 1; No = 0

Answer "Yes" if any laws or regulations grant different-sex and same-sex couples equal access to assisted reproductive technology.

Answer "No" if laws or regulations do not grant different-sex and same-sex couples equal access to assisted reproductive technology.

5.12. Do any laws or regulations grant different-sex and same-sex couples equal treatment regarding automatic co-parent recognition (that is, the same-sex partner of the parent who gives birth through medically assisted techniques is automatically recognized as the second parent)?

Yes = 1; No = 0
Yes = 1; No = 0

Answer "Yes" if any laws or regulations grant different-sex and same-sex couples equal treatment regarding automatic co-parent recognition (that is, the same-sex partner of the parent who gives birth through medically assisted techniques is automatically recognized as the second parent).

Answer "No" if no laws or regulations grant different-sex and same-sex couples equal treatment regarding automatic co-parent recognition.

5.13. Do any laws or regulations protect intersex persons (including children) from irreversible, nonemergency surgical or other medical interventions unless the intersex person has provided personal, free, and fully informed consent?

Yes = 1; No = 0
Yes = 1; No = 0

Answer "Yes" if any laws or regulations provide intersex persons (including children) with protection from irreversible, nonemergency surgical or other medical interventions unless the intersex person has provided personal, free, and fully informed consent.

Answer "No" if no laws or regulations protect intersex persons (including children) from irreversible, nonemergency surgical or other medical interventions unless the intersex person has provided personal, free, and fully informed consent.

5. Civil and political inclusion

5.14. Do any laws or regulations prohibit, ban, or protect against SOGIESC "conversion therapy"?   Yes = 1; No = 0

Answer "Yes" if any laws or regulations prohibit, ban, or protect against SOGIESC "conversion therapy."

Answer "No" if no laws or regulations prohibit, ban, or protect against SOGIESC "conversion therapy."

5.15. Do any clinical classifications provided by law or regulation categorize the following issues as a mental or physical disorder or pathologize the following?
- 5.15a. Being homosexual or bisexual   Yes = 0; No = 1
- 5.15b. Being transgender   Yes = 0; No = 1
- 5.15c. Being intersex   Yes = 0; No = 1

Answer "Yes" if clinical classifications provided by law or regulation categorize being homosexual or bisexual, transgender, or intersex as a mental or physical disorder or pathologize being homosexual or bisexual.

Answer "No" if no clinical classifications provided by law or regulation categorize being homosexual or bisexual, transgender, or intersex as a mental or physical disorder or pathologize being homosexual or bisexual.

5.16. Is persecution based on SOGIESC recognized as grounds for asylum?
- 5.16a. Sexual orientation   Yes = 1; No = 0
- 5.16b. Gender identity and expression   Yes = 1; No = 0
- 5.16c. Sex characteristics (intersex persons)   Yes = 1; No = 0

Answer "Yes" if persecution based on SOGIESC is recognized as grounds for asylum.

Answer "No" if persecution based on SOGIESC is not recognized as grounds for asylum.

6. Protection from hate crimes

6.1. Do any laws, constitutional provisions, or regulations criminalize hate crimes based on SOGIESC?

- 6.1a. Sexual orientation   Yes = 1; No = 0
- 6.1b. Gender identity and expression   Yes = 1; No = 0
- 6.1c. Sex characteristics (intersex persons)   Yes = 1; No = 0

Answer "Yes" if any laws, constitutional provisions, or regulations criminalize hate crimes based on SOGIESC.

Answer "No" if no laws, constitutional provisions, or regulations criminalize hate crimes based on SOGIESC.

6.2. Do any laws or regulations require government agencies to collect data on hate crimes committed against sexual and gender minorities or those perceived to be sexual or gender minorities?

- 6.2a. Sexual orientation   Yes = 1; No = 0
- 6.2b. Gender identity and expression   Yes = 1; No = 0
- 6.2c. Sex characteristics (intersex persons)   Yes = 1; No = 0

Answer "Yes" if any laws or regulations require government agencies to collect data on hate crimes committed against persons with diverse SOGIESC or those perceived as such.

Answer "No" if no laws or regulations require government agencies to collect data on hate crimes committed against persons with diverse SOGIESC or those perceived as such.

6.3. Are there mechanisms for monitoring and reporting hate crimes against sexual and gender minorities?

- 6.3a. Sexual orientation   Yes = 1; No = 0
- 6.3b. Gender identity and expression   Yes = 1; No = 0
- 6.3c. Sex characteristics (intersex persons)   Yes = 1; No = 0

Answer "Yes" if there are mechanisms for monitoring and reporting hate crimes against persons with diverse SOGIESC.

Answer "No" if there are no mechanisms for monitoring and reporting hate crimes against persons with diverse SOGIESC.

6.4. Is the commitment of a crime based on a person's SOGIESC considered an aggravating circumstance under the law?

- 6.4a. Sexual orientation — Yes ≡ 1; No ≡ 0
- 6.4b. Gender identity and expression — Yes ≡ 1; No ≡ 0
- 6.4c. Sex characteristics (intersex persons) — Yes ≡ 1; No ≡ 0

Answer "Yes" if the commitment of a crime based on a person's SOGIESC is considered an aggravating circumstance under the law.

Answer "No" if the commitment of a crime based on a person's SOGIESC is not considered an aggravating circumstance under the law.

6.5. Do any laws or policies mandate training the following professionals in recognizing and identifying hate crimes based on SOGIESC grounds?

- 6.5a. Police officers — Yes ≡ 1; No ≡ 0
- 6.5b. Prosecutors or judges — Yes ≡ 1; No ≡ 0
- 6.5c. Social workers — Yes ≡ 1; No ≡ 0
- 6.5d. Paramedics/doctors — Yes ≡ 1; No ≡ 0

Answer "Yes" if laws, regulations, or policies mandate training of police officers, prosecutors or judges, social workers, or paramedics or doctors in recognizing and identifying hate crimes based on SOGIESC grounds.

Answer "No" if laws, regulations, or policies do not mandate training of police officers, prosecutors or judges, social workers, or paramedics or doctors in recognizing and identifying hate crimes based on SOGIESC grounds.

6.6. Do any laws, constitutional provisions, or regulations mandate the provision of any of the following services to victims of hate crimes?

- 6.6a. Legal assistance — Yes ≡ 1; No ≡ 0
- 6.6b. Shelter/housing — Yes ≡ 1; No ≡ 0
- 6.6c. Forensics or medical examinations or medical certificates — Yes ≡ 1; No ≡ 0

Answer "Yes" if any laws, constitutional provisions, or regulations criminalize hate crimes based on SOGIESC, and if the laws or regulations mandate the provision of legal assistance (including in completing asylum applications and court forms), shelter or housing, forensics or medical examinations, or medical certificates to victims of hate crimes based on SOGIESC grounds.

Answer "No" if no laws, constitutional provisions, or regulations criminalize hate crimes based on SOGIESC, and if the laws or regulations do not mandate the provision of legal assistance (including in completing asylum applications and court forms), shelter or housing, forensics or medical examinations, or medical certificates to victims of hate crimes based on SOGIESC grounds.

6.7. What are the main reasons for not reporting incidents of SOGIESC discrimination in your country?

6.7a. Nothing would happen or change	Not scored
6.7b. Not worth reporting it	Not scored
6.7c. Did not want to reveal my sexual or gender identity	Not scored
6.7d. Concerned that the incident would not have been taken seriously	Not scored
6.7e. Did not know how or where to report	Not scored
6.7f. Too much trouble	Not scored
6.7g. Dealt with the problem myself or with friends	Not scored
6.7h. Fear of intimidation by perpetrators	Not scored
6.7i. Lack of legal protection and harassment or nonaction by police	Not scored
6.7j. Other	Not scored

6. Protection from hate crimes

Appendix B
Scoring methodology

Introduction

The Equality of Opportunity for Sexual and Gender Minorities (EQOSOGI) score is constructed using the following steps: (1) coding of legal responses into a binary quantitative indicator, (2) quality control of the computed binary indicators, and (3) computation of indicator set scores and the EQOSOGI score.

First step

The first step in deriving the EQOSOGI score consists of transforming the legal responses for all 138 questions into binary quantitative responses (0/1). The legal questions were originally answered with a "Yes" or "No" response, with those responses then recoded into a 0/1 binary indicator where 1 denotes equality of opportunity for sexual and gender minorities in the corresponding question and 0 otherwise. To illustrate this point, consider question 1.2 "Are same-sex relations between consenting adults explicitly criminalized?" In this case, a "No" response would reflect equality of opportunity for sexual and gender minorities and as such should be coded as 1. Similarly, a "Yes" response for question 3.9 "Do any laws or regulations require workplaces to have inclusive facilities, such as gender-neutral toilets?" would be coded as 1. Refer to appendix A for a comprehensive list of all 138 questions and their coding rules.

Second step

To assess the quality and consistency of the computed binary responses, the variability in the distribution of each binary response was analyzed. Of particular attention were those responses with low or null variation because, from a statistical standpoint, they convey very little or no additional information to the scores. When a given question and its quantitative coding response have the same value for all countries, say 0, the resulting score (computed as described in step 3) would be the same regardless of whether the question is included. Similarly, when a given question has a value of 1 for all countries, the resulting score would be proportionally shifted and will not alter the order in the distribution of countries. However, the ultimate decision of keeping indicators with low or null variability rests on their legal relevance for assessing equality of opportunity for sexual and gender minorities, the criterion followed here. For example, despite low data variation among responses within the Protection from Hate Crimes indicator set, these questions remain in the data set as an example of good legal practice and with the aim of encouraging countries to adopt laws promoting the inclusion of intersex persons. The variability is assessed by examining the response for each question. As an adopted criterion, questions showing an average value of 0 to 0.05 or 0.95 to 1 are considered to have low variability. The online descriptive statistics appendix (refer to the QR code on page 103) reports these averages and related descriptive statistics for all 138 questions and their associated binary responses. These descriptive statistics do not show major concerns but confirm the presence of questions with low variability across the six indicator sets, which are kept because of their legal relevance.

Third step

After coding and performing quality control of the legal questions into binary indicators, the next step to obtain the EQOSOGI score involves calculating the indicator set scores. For each of the six indicator sets, the scores are defined as the simple average of the indicators present in each set. Formally, the score for indicator set g, denoted by $\overline{ISS}_g$, is defined as

$$\overline{ISS}_g = \frac{1}{n_g} \sum_{i=1}^{n_g} q_{gi} \qquad (B.1)$$

where n_g is the number of indicators within indicator set g, and q_{gi} is the binary indicator i belonging to indicator set g. Note that g can be seen as a set of six elements; that is, g = {Decriminalization, Access to Education, Access to Labor Markets, Access to Services and Social Protection, Civil and Political Inclusion, Protection from Hate Crimes}.

Finally, the EQOSOGI country score, denoted by $EQOSOGI$, is defined as the average of the indicator set scores $\overline{ISS}_g$. Formally,

$$EQOSOGI = \frac{1}{6} \sum_{g=1}^{6} \overline{ISS}_g. \qquad (B.2)$$

This two-step averaging process ensures equal weighting within and between indicator sets. Both the indicator set scores and the EQOSOGI score range from 0 to 1. An EQOSOGI score equal to 0 for a given country means that the country does not have de jure any regulatory framework in favor of equality of opportunity for sexual and gender minorities; by contrast, an EQOSOGI score equal to 1 for a given country means that the country has a regulatory framework for all six indicator sets favoring the equality of opportunities for sexual and gender minorities.

Traffic lights representation of EQOSOGI scores: Low, medium, and high

To facilitate discussion around the EQOSOGI score, the EQOSOGI team has adopted a "traffic light" classification system that includes levels of low, moderate, and high presence of regulatory frameworks favoring the equality of opportunities for sexual and gender minorities. This proposal is inspired by a similar categorization used in the *Human Development Report* (for more information, refer to UNDP 1999) related to the Human Development Index. Additionally, the choice of thresholds for determining a state or classification of countries based on an index is quite common.[1]

The scoring categories are as follows: low (below 0.3), moderate (between 0.3 and 0.6), or high (above 0.6) presence of regulatory frameworks favoring the equality of opportunities for sexual and gender minorities. Clearly, other possible representations are feasible, and the reader is welcome to try another approach because the report provides open data for reproducibility. Figure B.1 summarizes the steps involved in the computation of the EQOSOGI score.

FIGURE B.1

Steps involved in the computation of the EQOSOGI score

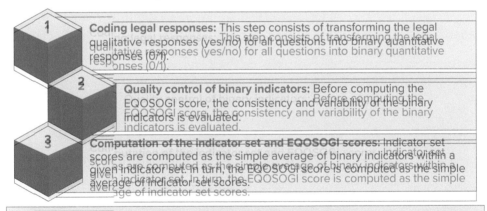

1. **Coding legal responses:** This step consists of transforming the legal qualitative responses (yes/no) for all questions into binary quantitative responses (0/1).

2. **Quality control of binary indicators:** Before computing the EQOSOGI score, the consistency and variability of the binary indicators is evaluated.

3. **Computation of the indicator set and EQOSOGI scores:** Indicator set scores are computed as the simple average of binary indicators within a given indicator set. In turn, the EQOSOGI score is computed as the simple average of indicator set scores.

"Traffic light" classification based on the EQOSOGI score: Based on their score, countries are classified as having either a low (below 0.3), moderate (between 0.3 and 0.6), or high (above 0.6) presence of regulatory frameworks favoring the equality of opportunities for sexual and gender minorities.

Source: Elaboration by the World Bank Equality of Opportunity for Sexual and Gender Minorities (EQOSOGI) team.

Illustration

Figure B.2 illustrates the construction of the EQOSOGI score for a hypothetical country. First, the answers to legal questions are coded into binary 0/1 indicators as shown for question 1.2. Next, the indicator set scores are computed as an average of the indicators included in the set, which leads to scores of 0.40 in Decriminalization,

FIGURE B.2

EQOSOGI score construction for a hypothetical country

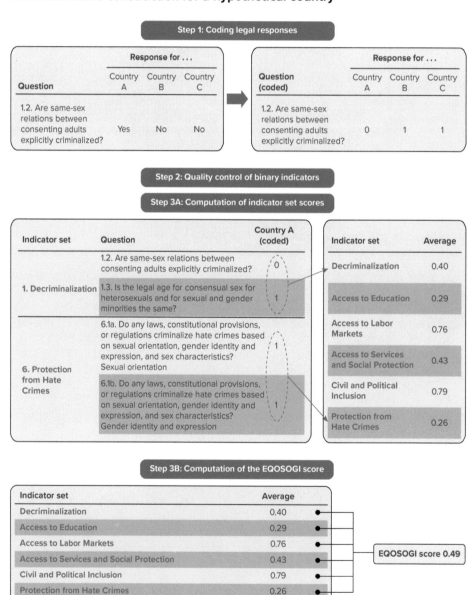

Source: World Bank Equality of Opportunity for Sexual and Gender Minorities (EQOSOGI) team.

0.29 in Access to Education, 0.76 in Access to Labor Markets, 0.43 in Access to Services and Social Protection, 0.79 in Civil and Political Inclusion, and 0.26 in Protection from Hate Crimes in this hypothetical country. Each of these values can be understood as a percentage of compliance in each indicator set. For example, this country has adopted 40 percent of the regulatory framework for decriminalizing sexual and gender minorities. Finally, the EQOSOGI score is computed as a simple average of these six values, which in this exercise is 0.49. This result indicates that this country offers about half of the total laws and/or regulations toward equality of sexual and gender minorities.

EQOSOGI scores by SOGIESC group

The EQOSOGI score, as well as the indicator set scores, are calculated for the three diverse sexual orientation, gender identity and expression, and sex characteristics (SOGIESC) groups: lesbian, gay, and bisexual; transgender; and intersex. It is important to consider that the legal questions used to construct the EQOSOGI score for each group may vary because some questions may specifically target a particular SOGIESC group. For example, question 1.1 "Do any laws or regulations explicitly criminalize people based on their diverse sexual orientation, gender identity and expression, and sex characteristics (SOGIESC)?" has three variants, each targeting a specific SOGIESC group. Specifically, variant 1.1a "Sexual orientation" refers to the lesbian, gay, and bisexual group, variant 1.1b "Gender identity and expression" refers to the transgender group, and variant 1.1c "Sex characteristics" refers to the intersex group. Table B.1 shows the list of questions used to construct the EQOSOGI score for each of the three SOGIESC groups. Questions in black are specific to the group, and questions in red are common across groups.

Comparison with the 2021 EQOSOGI scoring methodology

This report builds on the scoring methodology presented in the first EQOSOGI report (Cortez, Arzinos, and De la Medina Soto 2021). The 2024 report updates the EQOSOGI score in two ways. First, the 2024 version includes 51 additional questions (refer to table B.2). The addition of these questions enables the data to more accurately reflect the unique challenges that sexual and gender minorities experience in each of the six indicator sets. Sexual and gender minorities are not a homogenous group but are characterized by a wide range of experiences and barriers related to diverse SOGIESC. By disaggregating the data by group, this report allows for monitoring of

Equality of Opportunity for Sexual and Gender Minorities 2024

TABLE B.1

Selected questions to be used in the computation of the EQOSOGI score, by SOGIESC group

Selected questions to be used in the computation of the EQOSOGI score, by SOGIESC group

Indicator set	SOGIESC group		
	Lesbian, gay, and bisexual	Transgender	Intersex
Decriminalization	1.1a, 1.2, 1.3, 1.4a	1.1b, 1.4b, **1.5**, 1.6	1.1c, 1.4c, **1.5**
Access to Education	2.1a, 2.2a, 2.3a, **2.4, 2.5, 2.6, 2.7**	2.1b, 2.2b, 2.3b, **2.4, 2.5, 2.6, 2.7**, 2.8	2.1c, 2.2c, 2.3c, **2.4, 2.5, 2.6, 2.7**
Access to Labor Markets	3.1.1a, 3.1.2a, 3.2.1a, 3.2.2a, 3.3a, 3.4a, 3.5a, 3.6.1a, 3.6.2a, 3.7a, 3.8.1, 3.8.2	3.1.1b, 3.1.2b, 3.2.1b, 3.2.2b, 3.3b, 3.4b, 3.5b, 3.6.1b, 3.6.2b, 3.7b, **3.9, 3.10**	3.1.1c, 3.1.2c, 3.2.1c, 3.2.2c, 3.3c, 3.4c, 3.5c, 3.6.1c, 3.6.2c, 3.7c, **3.9**
Access to Services and Social Protection	4.1.1a, 4.1.2a, 4.1.3a, 4.2, 4.3a, 4.4a, 4.5a, 4.6a, 4.7a, 4.8a, 4.9a, **4.14**	4.1.1b, 4.1.2b, 4.1.3b, 4.3b, 4.4b, 4.5b, 4.6b, 4.7b, 4.8b, 4.9b, **4.12, 4.13, 4.14**	4.1.1c, 4.1.2c, 4.1.3c, 4.3c, 4.4c, 4.5c, 4.6c, 4.7c, 4.8c, 4.9c, 4.10a, 4.10b, **4.11, 4.12, 4.14**
Civil and Political Inclusion	**5.1, 5.2, 5.3**, 5.4a, 5.5a, 5.6, 5.7, 5.8, 5.9, 5.10, 5.11, 5.12, **5.14**, 5.15a, 5.16a	**5.1, 5.2, 5.3**, 5.4b, 5.5b, **5.14**, 5.15b, 5.16b	**5.1, 5.2, 5.3**, 5.4c, 5.5c, 5.13, 5.15c, 5.16c
Protection from Hate Crimes	6.1a, 6.2a, 6.3a, 6.4a, 6.5a, 6.5b, 6.5c, 6.5d, 6.6a, 6.6b, 6.6c	6.1b, 6.2b, 6.3b, 6.4b, 6.5a, 6.5b, 6.5c, 6.5d, 6.6a, 6.6b, 6.6c	6.1c, 6.2c, **6.3c, 6.4c, 6.5a**, 6.5b, 6.5c, 6.5d, 6.6a, 6.6b, 6.6c

Source: World Bank Equality of Opportunity for Sexual and Gender Minorities (EQOSOGI) team.
Note: Question numbers in **black** are specific to that group; question numbers in red are common across groups. SOGIESC = sexual orientation, gender identity and expression, and sex characteristics.

Source: World Bank Equality of Opportunity for Sexual and Gender Minorities (EQOSOGI) team.
Note: Question numbers in **black** are specific to that group; question numbers in red are common across groups. SOGIESC = sexual orientation, gender identity and expression, and sex charac

TABLE B.2

Number of questions in the EQOSOGI report, by indicator set, 2021 and 2024

Number of questions in the EQOSOGI report, by indicator set, 2021 and 2024

Indicator set	Number of questions	
	EQOSOGI Version 1	EQOSOGI Version 2
Decriminalization	4	10
Access to Education	7	14
Access to Labor Markets	12	34
Access to Services and Social Protection	26	37
Civil and Political Inclusion	23	24
Protection from Hate Crimes	15	19
Total	87	138

Source: World Bank Equality of Opportunity for Sexual and Gender Minorities (EQOSOGI) team.
Note: Version 1 refers to the EQOSOGI study comprising 16 countries published in 2021. Version 2 is the 2024 EQOSOGI report comprising 64 countries.

Source: World Bank Equality of Opportunity for Sexual and Gender Minorities (EQOSOGI) team.
Note: Version 1 refers to the EQOSOGI study comprising 16 countries published in 2021. Version 2 is the 2024 EQOSOGI report comprising 64 countries.

132

Appendix B: Scoring methodology

regional trends and disparities in legal protection for each group. Second, the calculation of the score uses a simple average to facilitate interpretation instead of the distance to the frontier approach used in the 2021 EQOSOGI report. The use of a simple average is in line with similar approaches used by World Bank flagship reports such as *Women, Business and the Law* (World Bank 2024). A limitation of the simple average is the use of equal weighting. From a legal perspective, some questions may be more or less important depending on the country and as such should have more or less weight in the calculation of the score.

Note

1. Refer to, for instance, the Heritage Foundation's Index of Economic Freedom, https://www.heritage.org/index/pages/country-pages/pakistan, and the Fund for Peace's Fragile States Index, https://fragilestatesindex.org/frequently-asked-questions/what-do-the-colors-and-categories-in-the-index-and-on-the-map-signify/#:~:text=Countries%20that%20score%20between%2030.0.and%20a%20colored%20light%20grey.

References

Cortez, E.; J. Arzinos, and C. De la Medina Soto. 2021. *Equality of Opportunity for Sexual and Gender Minorities*. Washington, DC: World Bank. http://hdl.handle.net/10986/36288.

UNDP (United Nations Development Programme). 1999. *Human Development Report 1999*. New York: Oxford University Press.

World Bank. 2024. *Women, Business and the Law 2024*. Washington, DC: World Bank.

Appendix C
Countries and local experts who contributed to the 2024 EQOSOGI

Introduction

This study was made possible by the generous contributions of lawyers, members of academia, representatives from civil society and nongovernmental organizations (NGOs), and advocates on sexual and gender minority issues from 64 countries. These contributions provided valuable information in response to the 138 questions of the Equality of Opportunity for Sexual and Gender Minorities (EQOSOGI) report for 2024. The following list provides the 64 countries that participated and the names of local experts and organizations wishing to be acknowledged individually.

Algeria
Aissa Amazigh, Mahabba Collective
Amal Hadjadj, *Le Journal Féministe Algérien*

Argentina
Javier Teodoro Álvarez, University of Buenos Aires
Angeles Bernachea, ECIJA Legal (Argentina)
María Bladimirsquy, University of Buenos Aires
Carlos Daniel Lafranconi, Deliberative Council of La Plata
María Julia Moreyrak, Peace Women Across the Globe
Denise Sanviti, Centro de Estudios de Política Internacional de la Universidad de Buenos Aires

Armenia
Mamikon Hovsepyan, Pink Human Rights Defender NGO
Varser Karapetyan, Human Rights House Yerevan
Melanie, DiverCity Social-Cultural, Human Rights Defender NGO
Queer Sista Platform Social-Cultural NGO

Bangladesh
Shale Ahmed, Bandhu Social Welfare Society
Md Masudur Rahman, BRAC
Md Mustakimur Rahman, Chinese University of Hong Kong

Equality of Opportunity for Sexual and Gender Minorities 2024

Bhutan

Wangda Dorji, Lhak-Sam (BNP+)/Bhutan Network of People Living with HIV and AIDS
Wangda Dorji, Lhak-Sam (BNP+)/Bhutan Network of People Living with HIV and AIDS
Tenzin Gyeltshen, Pride Bhutan
Tenzin Gyeltshen, Pride Bhutan
Lekey Khandu, Ministry of Health
Lekey Khandu, Ministry of Health

Brazil

Thiago Amaral, Attorney at Law
Thiago Amaral, Attorney at Law
Bianca Antacli, Tozzini Freire Advogados
Bianca Antacli, Tozzini Freire Advogados
Henrique Araujo, Cescon, Barrieu, Flesch & Barreto Advogados
Henrique Araujo, Cescon, Barrieu, Flesch & Barreto Advogados
Daniel Canavese, Federal Institute of Rio Grande do Sul
Daniel Canavese, Federal Institute of Rio Grande do Sul
Artur Carvalho, Tozzini Freire Advogados
Artur Carvalho, Tozzini Freire Advogados
Vinicius Castro, Cescon, Barrieu, Flesch & Barreto Advogados
Vinicius Castro, Cescon, Barrieu, Flesch & Barreto Advogados
Clara Clara Pacce Pinto Serva, Tozzini Freire Advogados
Clara Clara Pacce Pinto Serva, Tozzini Freire Advogados
Ana Paula Cristofolini, Cescon, Barrieu, Flesch & Barreto Advogados
Ana Paula Cristofolini, Cescon, Barrieu, Flesch & Barreto Advogados
Maria Custódio, Tozzini Freire Advogados
Maria Custódio, Tozzini Freire Advogados
Verônica Ennes Bastos de Araujo, Attorney at Law
Verônica Ennes Bastos de Araujo, Attorney at Law
Luiz Faria Jr., Tozzini Freire Advogados
Luiz Faria Jr., Tozzini Freire Advogados
Leonardo Lemos de Souza, State University of São Paulo
Leonardo Lemos de Souza, State University of São Paulo
Natalie Lima, Cescon, Barrieu, Flesch & Barreto Advogados
Natalie Lima, Cescon, Barrieu, Flesch & Barreto Advogados
Maurício Polidoro, Federal Institute of Rio Grande do Sul
Maurício Polidoro, Federal Institute of Rio Grande do Sul
Leticia Queiroz, Tozzini Freire Advogados
Leticia Queiroz, Tozzini Freire Advogados
Maitê Rezende, Cescon, Barrieu, Flesch & Barreto Advogados
Maitê Rezende, Cescon, Barrieu, Flesch & Barreto Advogados
Orlando Rios, Tozzini Freire Advogados
Orlando Rios, Tozzini Freire Advogados
Mário Saadi, Cescon, Barrieu, Flesch & Barreto Advogados
Mário Saadi, Cescon, Barrieu, Flesch & Barreto Advogados
Fernando Silva Teixeira Filho, State University of São Paulo
Fernando Silva Teixeira Filho, State University of São Paulo
Karina Silva, Tozzini Freire Advogados
Karina Silva, Tozzini Freire Advogados

Cambodia

Cameroon

Pencrace Bebga, Centre for Research on Peace, Environment and Governance (CREPEG)
Pencrace Bebga, Centre for Research on Peace, Environment and Governance (CREPEG)
Larissa Kojoue, Queer African Youth Network
Larissa Kojoue, Queer African Youth Network
Achille Kouyep, ACHREDHO Cameroun
Achille Kouyep, ACHREDHO Cameroun
George Lafon, Working for Our Wellbeing
George Lafon, Working for Our Wellbeing
Christian Damas Mintaka, Working for Our Wellbeing
Christian Damas Mintaka, Working for Our Wellbeing
Ebeneza Munkam Tchinfom, Cameroonian Foundation for AIDS (CAMFAIDS)
Ebeneza Munkam Tchinfom, Cameroonian Foundation for AIDS (CAMFAIDS)
Hamlet Nkwain, Working for Our Wellbeing
Hamlet Nkwain, Working for Our Wellbeing
Aristide Verlain Tchapon, ACHREDHO Cameroun
Aristide Verlain Tchapon, ACHREDHO Cameroun
Brice Tchuenguia, Working for Our Wellbeing
Brice Tchuenguia, Working for Our Wellbeing

Canada

Faisal Bhabda, York University
Faisal Bhabda, York University
André Capretti, HIV Legal Network
André Capretti, HIV Legal Network

Laura Cárdenas, IMK LLP
Barbara Findlay, The Law Office of Barbara Findlay KC
Hugo Lefebvre, IMK LLP
Johanna Macdonald, The 519
Nicole Simes, Simes Law
Amy Wah, HIV & AIDS Legal Clinic Ontario

Chile

Maria Francisca Bannura, Morales & Besa
Alexis Bulnes Troncoso, ONG Diversa Patagonia
Alejandro Chechilnitzky, Servicios Profesionales Guerrero Olivos Limitada
Israel Cortes Chavez, ONG Diversa Patagonia
Vicente Fleischmann, Morales & Besa
Ramón Gómez, Movilh, Movimiento de Integración y Liberación Homosexual
Mauricio Henriquez Rojas, Fundación Iguales
Raimundo Hurtado, Morales & Besa
Consuelo León, Morales & Besa
Sebastián Robles, Morales & Besa

China

Jia He, University of HK
Xi Huang, Trans Well-being Team
Darius Longarino, Yale Law School's Paul Tsai China Center

Costa Rica

Daniela Bolaños Torres, Centro de Investigación y Promoción para América Central de Derechos Humanos (CIPAC)
Natasha Jimenez, Mulabi
Francisco Jiménez Solano, independent legal practice
Michelle Jones Pérez, Arrecife
Argenis Ordoñez Garmendia, Costa Rican Ministry of Education
Daniel Arturo Valverde Mesén, ECIJA Legal (Costa Rica)
Jota Vargas

Côte d'Ivoire

Sheba Akpokli
Sylla Bouyeh Mahamadou
Bissa (Tia) Gossenin, Association Transgenres et Droits
Carlos Idiboue, Maison de la Culture des Diversités Humaines
Claver Toure, Alternative Côte d'Ivoire

Djibouti

Mélanie Guerinot, Cabinet d'avocat Mélanie Guerinot
Mohamed Omar Ibrahim

Ecuador

Paola Bermudez, Tesserae Bureau de Abogados
Causana
Pablo Crespo, Robalino Abogados Ecuador FEREC S.A.
María Gabriela Galeas, Probono Ecuador
Alexander Guano Monteros, Ministerio de la Mujer y Derechos Humanos en Ecuador
Carol Riofrio, Robalino Abogados Ecuador FEREC S.A.
Daniel Vásquez, Robalino Abogados Ecuador FEREC S.A.

Egypt, Arab Republic

Habiba Abdelaal
Egyptian Initiative for Personal Rights (EIPR)
Malak Elkashif, Transat MENA
Makarios Lahzy
Mostafa Mahmoud
Noor Sultan

Ethiopia

Fiji

Carlos Perera, University of the South Pacific
Renata Ram, Joint United Nations Programme on HIV/AIDS (UNAIDS)
Samuel Ram, Samuel K. Ram
Nalini Singh, Fiji Women's Rights Movement (FWRM)
Ana Tuiketei, Consultant—AP Legal
Laurel Vaurasi, Shekinah Law
Sulique Waqa, Haus of Khameleon

France

Christofer Adams, White & Case
Augustine Atry, Clinique Juridique de Lille
Salomé Gautret, Clinique Juridique de Lille
Nathanaël Griffart, Aix Global Justice
Guillemette Jegou, Clinique Juridique de Lille
Léo Laumonier, Laumonier Avocat
Ambre Marechal, Clinique Juridique de Lille
Caroline Mecary
Sophie Paricard, INU Champollion Albi
Quentin Pipieri, White & Case
Max Turner, White & Case

Georgia

Anri Abuladze, Tbilisi Pride
Ketevan Shubashvili, human rights lawyer

Germany

Hannah Berger, White & Case
German Institute for Human Rights
Julius Kalkofen, White & Case
Lesben- und Schwulenverband in Deutschland (LSVD)
Florian Rinnert, White & Case
Sophie Savoly, White & Case
Vincent Schreier, White & Case
Valérie Suhr, Universität Hamburg Fakultät für Rechtswissenschaft
Sara Vanetta, White & Case

Ghana

Sharon Ahlijah, Fugar & Company
Harper Caldwell, Human Rights Reporters Ghana (HRRG)
Mac-Darling Cobbinah, Centre for Popular Education and Human Rights (CEPEHRG)
Alex Kofi Donkor, LGBT+ Rights Ghana
Joseph Kobla Wemakor, Human Rights Reporters Ghana (HRRG)
Ebenezer Peegah, Rightify Ghana
Dedei Quarhsie, Centre for Popular Education and Human Rights (CEPEHRG)

Guinea-Bissau

José Paulo Costa de Jesus Cesário, United Nations Development Programme
(UNDP) Guinea-Bissau
Iaguba DJALO
J&L Advogados
ONG Nova Esperança
João Bernando Vieira

Guyana

Jermane Alleyne
Kesaundra Alves
Shivani Lalaram, Dentons
Tifaine Rutherford, Law Office of Tifaine Rutherford
Joel Simpson, SASOD

Haiti

Collectif d'Avocat.es Spécialisé.es en Litige Stratégique des Droits Humains (CALSDH)
Anderson Estimphil, Association KOURAJ
Niclene Jean-Baptiste, Femme En Action Contre la Stigmatisation et la
Discrimination Sexuelle (FACSDIS)
Edmide Joseph, Femme En Action Contre la Stigmatisation et la Discrimination
Sexuelle (FACSDIS)
Organisation Arc-en-Ciel d'Haiti (ORAH)

Equality of Opportunity for Sexual and Gender Minorities 2024

Vita Pierre
Vita Pierre
Edwige Saint-Louis, Femme En Action Contre la Stigmatisation et la Discrimination Sexuelle (FACSDIS)
Edwige Saint-Louis, Femme En Action Contre la Stigmatisation et la Discrimination Sexuelle (FACSDIS)
Jean Robens Theagene
Jean Robens Theagene

Honduras

Emanuel Salomon Bustillo Ponce, Defensoria Derechos Humanos
Emanuel Salomon Bustillo Ponce, Defensoria Derechos Humanos
Denis Ariel Díaz Cerrato, DYE Legal Firm
Denis Ariel Díaz Cerrato, DYE Legal Firm
Enrique Flores Rodríguez, Judiciary
Enrique Flores Rodríguez, Judiciary
Nadia Stefanía Mejía Amaya, Red Lésbica Cattrahas
Nadia Stefanía Mejía Amaya, Red Lésbica Cattrahas
Indyra María Mendoza Aguilar, Red Lésbica Cattrahas
Indyra María Mendoza Aguilar, Red Lésbica Cattrahas
Stephanye Michelle, Andino Ochoa
Stephanye Michelle, Andino Ochoa
Alex David Reyes, Consorcio Legal AJR
Alex David Reyes, Consorcio Legal AJR

India

Sarita Barpanda, Human Rights Law Network
Sarita Barpanda, Human Rights Law Network
Ryan Figueiredo, Equal Asia Foundation
Ryan Figueiredo, Equal Asia Foundation
Sonal Giani, IPPF South Asia Regional Office
Sonal Giani, IPPF South Asia Regional Office
Prashant Singh, Intersex Asia
Prashant Singh, Intersex Asia

Indonesia

Bella Aubree, Inti Muda Indonesia
Bella Aubree, Inti Muda Indonesia
Philo Dellano, PNB Law Firm
Philo Dellano, PNB Law Firm
M. Rizky Hady Eka Putra, Hiswara Bunjamin & Tandjung
M. Rizky Hady Eka Putra, Hiswara Bunjamin & Tandjung
Nursyahbani Katjasungkana, Indonesian Legal Aid Association for Women
Nursyahbani Katjasungkana, Indonesian Legal Aid Association for Women
Saskia Wieringa, Indonesian Legal Aid Association for Women
Saskia Wieringa, Indonesian Legal Aid Association for Women

Iraq

Fadak Nsaif, Salt & Associates
Fadak Nsaif, Salt & Associates
Zeyad Saeed, Iraqi law firm
Zeyad Saeed, Iraqi law firm
Tara Talabani
Tara Talabani

Israel

Vered Cainar, Orna Lin & Company
Vered Cainar, Orna Lin & Company
Nimrod Gornstein, independent expert and lecturer on lesbian, gay, bisexual, transgender, and queer public policy and law in Israel
Nimrod Gornstein, independent expert and lecturer on lesbian, gay, bisexual, transgender, and queer public policy and law in Israel
Yael Hershkovitz, Gissin & Company
Yael Hershkovitz, Gissin & Company
Ido Katri, Tel Aviv University
Ido Katri, Tel Aviv University
Ofer Kovacs, S. Horowitz & Company
Ofer Kovacs, S. Horowitz & Company
Or Levy
Or Levy
Rauda Morcos Rotem Sorek, Ma'avarim
Rauda Morcos Rotem Sorek, Ma'avarim
Imry Zagury, Aguda LGBTQ Israeli
Imry Zagury, Aguda LGBTQ Israeli

140

Jamaica

Nattecia Bohardsingh
Lorraine Francis, Cornell University
Maria Carla Gullotta, Stand Up for Jamaica
Glenroy Murray, Equality for All Foundation Jamaica
Kathryn Williams, Livingston, Alexander & Levy

Japan

Julien Bocobza, White & Case
Lucas Chen, White & Case
Yusuke Furukawa, White & Case
Maoko Kamiya, White & Case
Takeharu Kato, Hokkaido Godo Law Office
Ayako Kawano, White & Case
Tetsuro Kinoshita, Tokyo Kyodo Law Office
Makoto Koinuma, Greenberg Traurig Tokyo Law Offices
Yasuyuki Kuribayashi, City-Yuwa Partners
Yuki Mori, City-Yuwa Partners
Kiyoko Nakaoka, KUBOTA
Akira Nishiyama, Japan Alliance for LGBT Legislation, J-ALL
Koichiro Ohashi, Greenberg Traurig Tokyo Law Offices
Shizuka Onoyama, Junpo Law Office
Yuichiro Suzuki, KUBOTA
Mana Takahashi, Kanda University of International Studies
Yuki Takahashi, City-Yuwa Partners
Yusuke Watanabe, Greenberg Traurig Tokyo Law Offices

Jordan

Mohammed Al Nasser

Kenya

Rainbow Field, Bowmans
Lauriene Maingi, Cliffe Dekker Hofmeyr (incorporating Kieti Law)
Kivenzi Muange, galck+
Brian Muchiri, Cliffe Dekker Hofmeyr (incorporating Kieti Law)
Sammy Ndolo, Cliffe Dekker Hofmeyr (incorporating Kieti Law)
Clarice Wambua, Cliffe Dekker Hofmeyr (incorporating Kieti Law)

Korea, Republic of

Seung-Hyun Lee, Beyond the Rainbow Foundation
Ryan Thoreson, Human Rights Watch

Kosovo
Sarah Maliqi, Civil Rights Defenders
Ehat Miftaraj, Kosovo Law Institute
Gresa Rrahmani
Liridon Veliu, Center for Social Group Development

Kyrgyz Republic
Guliaim Aiylchy, Bishkek Feminist Initiative Team

Lebanon
Rima Al Mokdad, UN Women
Joelle Choueifati
Fadel Fakih, Lebanese Center for Human Rights
May Ghanem, UN Women
Strida Saghbiny, Seeds for Legal Initiatives
Lama Sakr
Layal Sakr, Seeds for Legal Initiatives
Dalal Yassine, Middle East Voices

Mauritius
Anjeelee Kaur Beegun, UKI Consultancy Services
Nansha Bholah
Najeeb A. Fokeerbux, Young Queer Alliance
Shatyam Raze Issur, Collectif Urgence Toxida
Danisha Sornum, Leadinclude Africa

Mexico
Ephraem Adamtey, White & Case
Marco Antonio Del Toral Morales, United Nations Office on Drugs and Crime (UNODC)
Javiera Yanina Donoso Jiménez
Fernando Elizondo García, Tecnológico de Monterrey
Amara García-Pensamiento, SCJN
Adalberto Méndez López, ECIJA Legal (Mexico)

Mongolia
Gal-Ariun Bayaraa, Nomin & Advocates
Nomin Dashnyam, MahoneyLiotta LLP
Zoljargal Dashnyam, DB & GTS
Erdeneburen Dorjpurev, LGBT Centre of Mongolia
Enkhmaa Enkhbold, LGBT Centre of Mongolia
Dorjjantsan Ganbaatar, LGBT Centre of Mongolia

Saranzaya Gerelt-od, Asian Development Bank
Munkhzul Khurelbaatar, NHRCM
Munkhjargal Munkhbat, MJL Attorneys
Legee Tamir, YouthLEAD
Otgonbaatar Tsedendemberel, Corvinus University of Budapest

Morocco
Salima Bakouchi, Bakouchi & Habachi—HB Law Firm
Naoufal Bouzid
Fatiha Chtatou, Union Féministe Libre
Kamal Habachi, Bakouchi & Habachi—HB Law Firm
Saad Morchid, Bakouchi & Habachi—HB Law Firm
Nassawiyat

Mozambique
Tarik Azize, Kutchindja Association
Dário De Sousa, LAMBDA
Pepetsa Fumo, TRANSformar.moz
Gimina Langa, SAL & Caldeira Advogados, Lda
Deisy Massango, Foundation for Community Development
Celvicta Munguambe, SAL & Caldeira Advogados, Lda

Nepal
Sangeet Kayastha, YPEER Asia Pacific Center & Disabilities2030
Subin Mulmi, Nationality for All
Prapoosa KC, Green Law Associates
Anuj Petter Rai, Blue Diamond Society
Esan Regmi, Campaign for Change, Nepal
Sarita KC, Mitni Nepal
Medha Sharma, Visible Impact
Surendra Tiwari, Imperial Law Associates

New Zealand
Vinod Bal, Adhikaar Aotearoa
Marie Bismark, University of Melbourne
Duncan Matthews, Rule Foundation
Frankie Karetai Wood-Bodley, Karetai Wood-Bodley & Co.

Nigeria
Emmanuel Abraye, Perchstone & Graeys
Oghomwen Akpaibor, Templars Law Firm
Olamide Aleshinloye, Udo Udoma & Belo-Osagie

Equality of Opportunity for Sexual and Gender Minorities 2024

Oluwakemi Awoniyi, Arthur Nylander Chambers
Oluwakemi Awoniyi, Arthur Nylander Chambers
Chidinma Chukwuma, Udo Udoma & Belo-Osagie
Chidinma Chukwuma, Udo Udoma & Belo-Osagie
Folabi Kuti, Perchstone & Graeys
Folabi Kuti, Perchstone & Graeys
Beulah Lekwauwa, Perchstone & Graeys
Beulah Lekwauwa, Perchstone & Graeys
Victoria Ngozi, Human Development Initiatives
Victoria Ngozi, Human Development Initiatives
Leslie Nylander, Arthur Nylander Chambers
Leslie Nylander, Arthur Nylander Chambers
Anthony Obidike, Perchstone & Graeys
Anthony Obidike, Perchstone & Graeys
Ozofu Ogiemudia, Udo Udoma & Belo-Osagie
Ozofu Ogiemudia, Udo Udoma & Belo-Osagie
Tanimola Oyekan, Perchstone & Graeys
Tanimola Oyekan, Perchstone & Graeys
Ayomide Soretire, Udo Udoma & Belo-Osagie
Ayomide Soretire, Udo Udoma & Belo-Osagie
Inam Wilson, Templars Law Firm
Inam Wilson, Templars Law Firm

Norway

Lars Arnesen, University of Oslo
Lars Arnesen, University of Oslo
Ane Bergo, Advokatfirma DLA Piper Norway DA
Ane Bergo, Advokatfirma DLA Piper Norway DA
Isak Bradley, Patient Organization for Gender Incongruence
Isak Bradley, Patient Organization for Gender Incongruence
Warvin Einkjøb, Equality and Anti-Discrimination Ombud
Warvin Einkjøb, Equality and Anti-Discrimination Ombud
Maja Elgaaen, Lawfirm Helmr
Maja Elgaaen, Lawfirm Helmr
Erik Råd Herlofsen, Lawfirm Helmr
Erik Råd Herlofsen, Lawfirm Helmr
Miriam Kveen, Equality and Anti-Discrimination Ombud
Miriam Kveen, Equality and Anti-Discrimination Ombud
Lene Løvdal, Egalia Centre against Discrimination
Lene Løvdal, Egalia Centre against Discrimination
Elin Mack Løvdal, Advokatfirmaet CLP DA
Elin Mack Løvdal, Advokatfirmaet CLP DA
Linnea Mathieu, Lawfirm Helmr
Linnea Mathieu, Lawfirm Helmr
Bjørg Norli, Pro Sentret
Bjørg Norli, Pro Sentret
Elsa Sjong-Arnestad, FRI—Norwegian Organization for Sexual and
    Gender Diversity
Elsa Sjong-Arnestad, FRI—Norwegian Organization for Sexual and
    Gender Diversity
Cecilie Sjursen, Advokatfirmaet CLP DA
Cecilie Sjursen, Advokatfirmaet CLP DA
Harald Strømstad, Advokatfirma DLA Piper Norway DA
Harald Strømstad, Advokatfirma DLA Piper Norway DA
Andrea Vige Grønningsæter, Faculty of Law, University of Oslo
Andrea Vige Grønningsæter, Faculty of Law, University of Oslo
Ingun Wik, Public Health Centre for Gender and Sexuality, Municipality of Oslo
Ingun Wik, Public Health Centre for Gender and Sexuality, Municipality of Oslo

Pakistan

Zubair Faisal Abbasii, IMPACT—Research International
Zubair Faisal Abbasii, IMPACT—Research International
Yasser Latif Hamdani
Yasser Latif Hamdani
Uzma Yaqoob, Forum for Dignity Initiative (FDI)
Uzma Yaqoob, Forum for Dignity Initiative (FDI)

Papua New Guinea

Stephen Massa, Dentons PNG
Stephen Massa, Dentons PNG
Emma Minimbi, Roni Pingrui Community Development Association Inc
Emma Minimbi, Roni Pingrui Community Development Association Inc
Patience Pip, TotalEnergies EP PNG Limited
Patience Pip, TotalEnergies EP PNG Limited
Iru Tau, Kapul Champions
Iru Tau, Kapul Champions

Philippines

Eva Aurora Callueng, University of the East
Claire De Leon, LAGABLAB LGBT Network
Jap Paul Jann Ignacio, Babaylanes, Inc.
Ryan Silverio, ASEAN SOGIE Caucus
Juan Carlo Tejano, Sentro ng Alternatibong Lingap Panlegal (SALIGAN)
Michael Tiu, Jr., UB Gender Law and Policy Program

Serbia

Dragisa Calic, Lawyer's Committee for Human Rights (YUCOM)
Agata Milan Đurić, Geten—Center for LGBTIQA People's Rights
Katarina Golubovic, Lawyer's Committee for Human Rights (YUCOM)
Ivana Jovanović, Youth Initiative for Human Rights
Vuk Raičević, Belgrade Centre for Human Rights
Kristian Ranđelović, XY Spectrum
Dejana Stosic, Youth Initiative for Human Rights
Maja Žilić, Youth Initiative for Human Rights

South Africa

Bonga Dentshe, White & Case
Joseph Harries, White & Case
Ayesha-Bibi Karjieker, Cliffe Dekker Hofmeyr Inc
Charlene Kreuser, Legal Resources Centre
Nadeem Mahomed, Cliffe Dekker Hofmeyr Inc
Khuliso Managa, Women's Legal Centre
Brigitta Mangale, Cliffe Dekker Hofmeyr Inc
Charlene May, Women's Legal Centre
Letlhogonolo Mokgoroane, Centre for Applied Legal Studies
Kayla Moodley, White & Case
Khensani Motileni, Women's Legal Centre
Jodie Muller, White & Case
Ewa Orpen, White & Case
Amy-Leigh Payne, Legal Resources Centre
Elgene Roos, Cliffe Dekker Hofmeyr Inc
Sheena Swemmer, Centre for Applied Legal Studies

Spain

Rodrigo Araneda Villasante, ACATHI: migración, refugio y diversidad LGBTIQ+
Graziano Ceccheti, Giambrone & Partners
Diego Hernández-Sampelayo, White & Case
Tim Hope, White & Case
Coral Nevaldos, Giambrone & Partners

Carlos Peña Cifuentes, White & Case
Marina Saenz, Ministry of Justice
Laia Silvia Busquet, Giambrone & Partners
Yoko Takagi, White & Case
Miguel Vieito Villar, Miguel Vieito—Avogado
Gines Zamora, Adalium Abogados

Sri Lanka
Rosanna Flamer Caldera, Equal Ground
Niluka Perera, Diversity and Solidarity Trust (DAST)
John Wilson, John Wilson Partners, Attorneys-at-Law and Notaries Public

Sudan
Ahmed ElHillali
Noor Sultan

Tanzania
Bronnina and Clarissa
Arnold Nicholaus, KVP Forum Tanzania
Mwamba T. Nyanda, Tanzania Trans Initiative
Salum

Thailand
APCOM Foundation
Patcharanon Bumroongsook, A&O Shearman
Nada Chaiyajit
Ryan Joseph Figueiredo, Equal Asia Foundation
Jose Herrera, Herrera & Partners
Dr. Rapeepun Jommaroeng, Rainbow Sky Association of Thailand (RSAT)
Jawying Honey Lyster, United Nations Development Programme (UNDP)
Dr. Timo T. Ojanen

Timor-Leste
Jose Tomas Alves, Miranda & Associados, Sociedade de Advogados, SP, RL
Nuria Brinkman, Miranda & Associados, Sociedade de Advogados, SP, RL
Susana Pinto Coelho, Miranda & Associados, Sociedade de Advogados, SP, RL
Monica Mendes da Silva, MDS Legal, Lda.
Laura Afonso De Jesus, Coalition for Diversity Action (CODIVA)
Ana Paula Marçal, Judicial System Monitoring Programme
Elisa Pereira, Abreu e C&C Advogados Timor-Leste
Luis Ximenes, NGO Belun
Ying Hooi Khoo, Universiti Malaya

Tunisia

Chedi Berrich, Juridika Conseil
Insaf Bouhafs, Avocats Sans Frontières
Henda Chennaoui
Nessryne Jelalia
Houyem Mchirgui, The Initiative Mawjoudin for Equality
Ramla Yakoubi, Juridika Conseil

Türkiye

Kerem Dikmen, Kaos GL (Kaos Gay and Lesbian Cultural Research and Solidarity
    Association)
Kardelen Yılmaz, May 17 Association
Sena Yılmaz, Social Policy Gender Identity and Sexual Orientation Studies
    Association

Ukraine

Iryna Boiko, Ukrainian Center of Legal Studies
Olha Podilchak, Ukrainian Center of Legal Studies
Anna Sharyhina, NGO Women Association Sphere (Kharkiv, Ukraine)
Olena Shostko, Ukrainian Center of Legal Studies
Denys Sytnyk, Sytnyk & Partners LLC
Anastasiia Yeva Domani, Cohort
Aleksandra Yevstafyeva, EPAP Ukraine

Uruguay

José Fabeiro, Ferrere Abogados
Lucía Fernández Ramírez, APTA Asesoramiento y Consultoría
Daniela Jaunarena, Ferrere Abogados
Isabel Laventure, Ferrere Abogados
Marcela Schenck, Universidad de la República
Diego Sempol, Universidad de la República
Rodrigo Simaldone, United Nations Educational, Scientific and Cultural Organization
    (UNESCO)
Gabriel Valentin, Instituto Uruguayo de Derecho Procesal
Alvaro Xavier de Mello, ECIJA Legal (Uruguay)

Viet Nam

Tu-Anh Hoang, Center for Creative Initiatives in Health and Population
Phong Vuong Kha, Institute for Studies of Society, Economy & Environment (iSEE)
Pham Duy Khuong, ASL Law
Nguyen Thi Thuy Chung, ASL Law
Pham Thanh Truc, RHTLaw Vietnam

Equality of Opportunity for Sexual and Gender Minorities 2024

Zimbabwe

Carole Bamu, Bamu Attorneys
Carole Bamu, Bamu Attorneys
Roselyn Hanzi, Zimbabwe Lawyers for Human Rights
Roselyn Hanzi, Zimbabwe Lawyers for Human Rights
Natalie Jenami, Bamu Attorneys
Natalie Jenami, Bamu Attorneys
Alex Farai Majachani, Alex F and Associates Attorneys
Alex Farai Majachani, Alex F and Associates Attorneys
Chesterfield Samba, GALZ
Chesterfield Samba, GALZ
Vivian Vengeyi, Alex F and Associates Attorneys
Vivian Vengeyi, Alex F and Associates Attorneys

www.ingramcontent.com/pod-product-compliance
Lightning Source LLC
Chambersburg PA
CBHW040700160225
22018CB00020B/386